Trackside Scenes

You Can Model

JIM KELLY

KALMBACH BOOKS

© 2003 Kalmbach Publishing Co. All rights reserved. This book may not be reproduced in part or in whole without written permission of the publisher, except in the case of brief quotations used in reviews. Published by Kalmbach Publishing Co., 21027 Crossroads Circle, Waukesha, WI 53187.

Printed in the United States of America

03 04 05 06 07 08 09 10 11 12   10 9 8 7 6 5 4 3 2 1

For more information, visit our website at http://www.kalmbach.com

Publisher's Cataloging in Publication
(Provided by Quality Books, Inc.)

Kelly, Jim, 1940-
    Trackside scenes you can model / Jim Kelly.
    p. cm.
    Includes bibliographical references and index.
    ISBN 0-89024-423-5

    1. Railroads—Models. 2. Landscape. 3. Miniature craft. I. Title.

TF197.K455 2003   625.1'9
                          QBI03-2--627

Art Director: Kristi Ludwig
Book design: Mark Watson

Contents

Welcome aboard 4

Arrivals and departures: railroad yards
    An "A-okay" yard in Ardmore: An ideal prototype with only five tracks ..6
    A towerman's view at Bakersfield: Beautifully weathered track 8
    A tale of two bridges: Breaking up a yard's linearity 10
    Sorting it all out: A Kentucky coal-marshalling yard 12
    Loading pigs: Basic ingredients of an intermodal hub 14
    Modeling past and present: An easy-to-build yard office 15
    Caboose for supplies: Convert old equipment into storage sheds 16

Care and feeding: enginehouses and terminals
    Keep 'em moving: A simple diesel service facility 18
    Fill 'er up: Butler, Pa., fuel dock 21
    Laying off in Ludlow: A contemporary diesel servicing facility 22
    The one and only: An enginehouse built as solid as a rock 23
    Small, yet significant: A pocket-sized enginehouse 24
    Shelter without substance: C&IM's single-stall enginehouse 26
    Down and dirty: A steel-sheathed enginehouse in decline 28

Staying above it all: bridges
    Arches and flyovers: Spanning the Susquehanna 30
    Flying high: Cascade bridge features towering steel trestles 38
    High up on the MR&T: Kitbashing a high steel trestle 40
    Looking west: More high trestles 41
    They're everywhere: Deck girder bridges 42
    Whatever is is right: Combination bridges 44
    Crossing with a twist: East Dubuque's iron truss & swing bridges 45
    Serving Huckleberry's hometown: Three generations of bridges 52

The battle against monotony: tunnels and shelf scenes
    Now you see it, now you don't: SP's tunnels at Tehachapi 56
    Up against the wall: The perfect mountain scene 60

Along the line
    Round in circles we go: The Tehachapi Loop 66
    Ace of diamonds: Rochelle Railroad Park 71
    On the edge: Station at Bridgeport, Wis. 75

Three guiding principles: form, color, and texture 77

Suppliers mentioned in this book (and some others) 78

Suggested reading 79

Index 80

Welcome aboard

This book was Dick Christianson's idea. (Dick is *Model Railroader* Magazine's managing editor—again—but was head of the Kalmbach Books Department when we embarked on the project.) The premise was to choose railroad photos that model railroaders would find interesting and write about them. Beyond that, the approach was all up to me. All that freedom made it tough in the beginning, but fun once I got started.

I've used several dozen of my own photos, but mostly I've relied on those taken by others. Because I am a retired managing editor of *Model Railroader* Magazine, I have had access to Kalmbach Publishing Company's photo library and, even more importantly, access to a lot of fertile minds at Kalmbach and across the country.

This, then, is a book of model railroading ideas and philosophy. I hope you'll find some concepts and inspiration here to get your own wheels turning, both those in your head and those on your locomotives.

I've tried to cover a lot of bases here, particularly those features most modelers want: bridges, tunnels, and railroad yards. I've offered my ideas on different kinds of scenery and hints on how to model them. This is not a rigid reference book though, and so, if a bridge shows up in a photo in the tunnel section, it'll be discussed there (or maybe it won't). This is a book you could read from cover to cover, or one you could just poke around in.

Some of you may find entire scenes here you want to model (the Bridgeport, Wis., river scene or the Detroit, Toledo & Ironton's Jackson, Ohio, engine terminal come to mind), but I imagine most of you will be looking for snippets from the scenes that would work out well for you. I can't imagine any of you would model the Pennsylvania's Rockville bridge in its entirety, but it has many interesting individual features that you could borrow.

My own approach to model railroading is prototype-inspired. I like to model the scenery and structures of Tehachapi Pass as they were in 1983, but I compress, leave things out, and don't hesitate to add something if it seems appropriate. In my mind I'm sometimes improving on what the railroad really did. It's a model railroad for the enjoyment of me and my friends, not a historical museum piece.

At the same time I'm a champion of plausibility. True enough, it's your railroad and you can do anything you want. At the same time, I think you'll have more fun if your railroad is based on how railroads really went about their business. And you'll be more satisfied with your bridges, tunnels, rights-of-way, and all the rest if you know they make sense prototypically. They'll just "look right."

I've included some ideas on kits and materials you could use for certain projects, but there are certainly others I may not have thought of or known about. Every time I thumb through a Walthers catalog products jump out I've never noticed before.

I had a lot of help with this book. Thank you so much to Tom Danneman, George Drury, Cody Grivno, Jim Hediger, Dave Ingles, Kent Johnson, Rob McGonigal, Hal Miller, David Popp, Chuck Porter, Gil Reid, John Roberts, Andy Sperandeo, Carl Swanson, and Terry Thompson.

If you enjoy this book, that's wonderful and I'll take a bow. If you don't—hey, it was Dick's idea!
-Jim Kelly

Trackside Scenes

You Can Model

RAILROAD YARDS

Hal Miller

An "A-okay" yard
An ideal prototype with only five tracks

This journey through a hundred or so railroad photographs has to begin somewhere, so why not on a peaceful evening in August 1993 at the Santa Fe yard in Ardmore, Oklahoma. The furnace-like heat has gone from the air and there's a pleasant breeze.

The nice thing about this yard, from a model railroading point of view, is its size. As yards go, it's small, about the size most modelers have room for. Assuming the locomotive is on the main line, we have five classification tracks, and that's about right. We can use one class track for spotting cars that have come in from the north, another for cars that have come in from the south, one for cars that will be going out to the north, and another for those that will be heading south. We can use the fifth track for sorting, making up locals, and other duties.

The main line swings to our right as it approaches the foreground, leaving the yard with a lead (also called "drill track") to our left that isn't fouled by main-line trains. Often it's neglected, but you need a drill track, and it needs to be as long as your yard tracks. Finding a place for it can be tough (especially if you didn't plan for it from the beginning). Usually the

Ardmore, Okla., is served by the Santa Fe. The grain elevator and southwestern-style station have a lot to recommend them, and so does this "right-sized" freight yard.

most workable solution is to have it run parallel with the main line.

A good trick for differentiating between the main and the drill tracks is to use different ballast colors. This may sound a bit artificial, but in fact you'll see it often on real railroads. The main line rates the more-expensive crushed rock and is tweaked and cleaned more often. The yards and spurs get the less-expensive stuff, which in

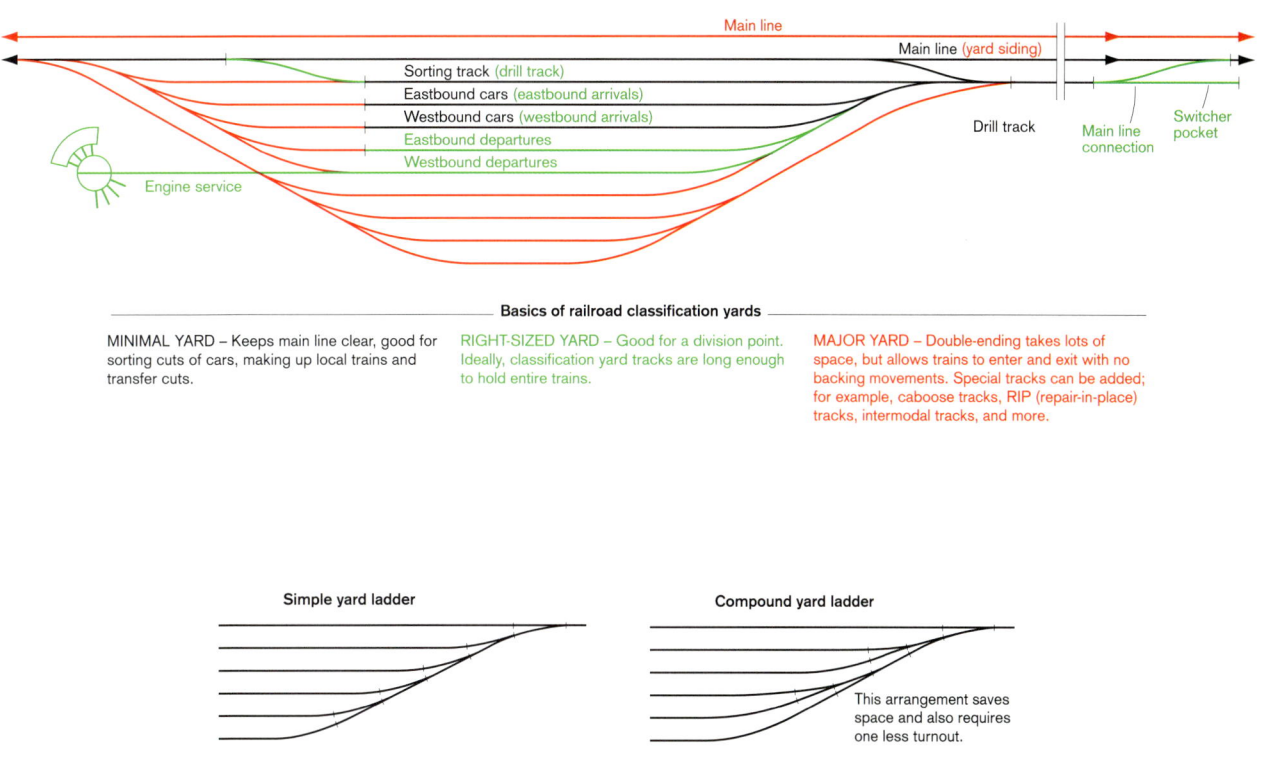

steam days was often coal cinders, and they receive less maintenance. Following this prototype lead will make your layout more comprehendible to operators and visitors.

Among the interesting details we see at Ardmore is the service road crossing the yard throat. If a pickup truck is blocked by a train here, it'll be one that's moving (or about to be) and will soon be out of the way. Note also the broad parking and access area to the left. Your workers need to be able to get to the job.

The ultimate reference for any model railroader wanting to plan a yard is John Armstrong's classic book, *Track Planning for Realistic Operation*, published by Kalmbach Publishing Co. One thing you would learn there is that the yard throat turnout arrangement seen at Ardmore is simple, and that the Santa Fe could have saved space by using a compound arrangement. See the diagram above. Of course the Santa Fe had a lot more room in and around Ardmore than you do in your basement.

Yards come in all shapes and sizes, depending on the jobs they need to do. On the prototype they evolve constantly as the equipment, business, and traffic patterns change. For example, at the Santa Fe's Bakersfield, Calif., yard (shown in the next chapter) some of those tracks that once served icing docks for refrigerator cars were removed, and others were put to work handling intermodal loading.

I'm including a drawing here that suggests how a yard can be sized to a layout. You start with the basics, shown in black, and can plan for a bigger yard, adding the green tracks. Adding the red tracks gives you a major yard but will take lots of space. Look to the prototype and Mr. Armstrong for further ideas.

RAILROAD YARDS

Jim Kelly

A towerman's view

Beautifully weathered track

Bakersfield Yard may be too large to model in its entirety, but we can pick up some interesting detailing tips here. The mainline tracks are to the right; note that the ballast used on them is a lighter color. If you could get closer, you'd also see that the mainline ballast is better maintained, and there's a lot more of it.

Note the oil and grease stains centered between the rails of the yard tracks. We can also see small whitish piles of material here and there along the rail. These are probably sand leaked by locomotive sanding pipes as engines sat for a considerable while, but they could also be fertilizer or other cargo slowly leaked from cars. The important thing is that they're a simple detail we could add to make our yard tracks more realistic.

Another detail is that golf-cart-sized grade crossing just below the middle of the photo. Notice that it turns right and there's room enough between the tracks here for a yard worker to go out checking for car numbers or inspecting car wheels.

In the distance (and not easy to see here) is a long highway bridge that carries traffic over the yard. It was a great place to watch roundhouse activity before the roundhouse was torn down in the late 1980s, but for a model railroad it would serve a very important visual function. Because yards are so long and take up so much space, they tend to be dull

This view of the Santa Fe yard at Bakersfield, Calif., photographed in May 1983, explains at a glance why most model railroaders can't incorporate major yards into their layouts. They're just too durned big. Bakersfield yard is some two miles long.

and without centers of visual attention (which boxcar are you supposed to look at?). Given that, any bridges that cross yards break up the linearity and add interest, even more so if they cross at an angle. Rix highway overpasses are perfect for this, and the company makes them in both HO and N scales. You have your choice of a vintage (1930s– '40s) or a modern bridge.

On most layouts, such bridges

are usually perpendicular to the aisles and come right out to the edges, so they offer choice in-your-face locations for displaying your best highway vehicles.

You can also relieve the visual sameness of a yard with footbridges. They can simply go from one area to another and don't have to cross the yard completely. Elevated steam pipes or other piping are also good for breaking up the monotony of parallel tracks.

And your yard tracks don't have to be equally spaced. Some might be further apart to allow for a road or a track that's been removed.

A model of a tower like the one at Bakersfield would serve very nicely to break up the humdrum of your railyard. Basically it's a typical two-story railroad signal tower on stilts. American Ltd., Bachmann, and Walthers offer plastic kits that would lend themselves well to this project, and Sheepscot has a dandy tower in a wood craftsman kit.

N scalers could use Dimi Trains no. 2010, a gem of a plastic kit which I intend to use for this model (and have been so intending for nearly 20 years) or a wood craftsman kit from American Model Builders (no. 602) or Showcase (no. 112).

Wood, etched-brass, and cast-metal staircases are available in both HO and N. Both Evergreen and Plastruct make plastic structural shapes you could use, and these are also available in brass from K&S and Special Shapes. Have fun with it, and if you make an extra one in N, you know whom to call.

A centrally located yard tower would help ease the monotony of any model railroad yard.

Your workers would appreciate relief from the cold.

Incidentally, that tiny structure next to the Bakersfield yard tower is a warm-up shed, and here's a photo of its interior. The piping left of the old cast-iron stove suggests it's been converted to gas or oil. Grandt Line makes an old-fashioned stove in HO and Period Miniatures has one in N.

KEY MATERIALS

Highway overpasses
Rix in HO and N

Tower models
American Ltd., Bachmann, and Walthers plastic kits
Sheepscot wood craftsman kit
Dimi Trains no. 2010 (N scale)
American Model Builders (no. 602) or Showcase (no. 112) wood craftsman kits

Details/Materials
Wood, etched-brass, and cast-metal staircases in both HO and N
Structural shapes in plastic: Evergreen and Plastruct
Structural shapes in brass: K&S and Special Shapes
Old-fashioned stove: Grandt Line in HO and Period Miniatures in N

RAILROAD YARDS

Keith Thompson

A tale of two bridges

Breaking up a yard's linearity

Butler Yard (now Union Pacific property) is named for the city in which it is located: Butler, Wis., located just west of the Milwaukee city limits. The yard offices, middle of the photo, are typical of those found in large, modern yards. You could combine a Pikestuff no. 5005 multi-purpose steel building with one of their no. 16 yard office kits to make a similar office complex. The N scale equivalents are nos. 8005 and 8001.

A Chicago & North Western unit coal train rolls through the C&NW's Butler Yard in May 1994.

Keith Thompson took this photo from the Hampton Ave. overpass, a favorite haunt of Milwaukee area railfans. He's looking south.

Here again is support for that old adage, "Take your pictures while you can." The yard is still there, but the offices have been torn down.

KEY MATERIALS

Steel buildings
Pikestuff no. 5005 multi-purpose steel building (HO), 8005 (N)
Pikestuff yard office kits, no. 16 (HO) and no. 8001 (N)

Bridge (HO)
Central Valley no. 19025 bridge girder sections
Micro Engineering girders
Evergreen I beams, channels, and columns

Modern overpass
Rix in HO and N

The early Hampton Ave. overpass (right) was substantial enough to do the job, but it was certainly a rickety-looking affair from the ground and would make a great prototype for a highway overpass set in the 1960s or earlier. You could make the trestle bents from either styrene or wood. A homemade jig would make the job go faster. For building the through-girder bridge in HO, you could use several packages of Central Valley no. 19025 bridge girder sections, some Micro Engineering girders, and some I beams, channels, and columns from Evergreen.

Bear in mind that highway bridges are generally quite a bit lighter and lacier than railroad bridges, and for a simple reason: automobiles and trucks don't weigh near as much as trains. Making your highway bridges a little on the scrawny side will make your railroad bridges look all the more businesslike.

Jochen E. Dreschler

The Hampton Ave. overpass as it looked when photographed in 1969.

Jochen E. Dreschler

The pre-1969 Hampton Ave. bridge was totally devoid of architectural merit. The angles at the ends of the through-truss portion don't even match. Back then, Butler and points west were still "a ways out" from Milwaukee, and there wasn't nearly as much highway traffic as there is today.

The pre-1969 Hampton Ave. bridge as seen from the south.

When your author took this shot, he was probably more interested in the old C&NW GP-7 that had been sold to the Fox River Valley Railroad. Nonetheless, you get a good view of the underpinnings of today's Hampton Ave. overpass. One of Rix's modern overpasses would represent it very nicely.

The modern Hampton Avenue overpass, photographed in April 1991.

Jim Kelly

RAILROAD YARDS

John Roberts

Sorting it all out

A Kentucky coal-marshalling yard

Basically, a coal-marshalling yard is like any other yard—it's just more specialized. Local coal trains work up and down the mountain hollows and haul coal back from the various mines. At the marshalling yard, the loaded cars are assembled (marshalled) into longer cross-country trains, and the incoming empties are divvied out.

Here again you see lighter ballast on the main line. Note that the ties are practically buried in it. This might be a realistic touch but, in my experience, modeling it doesn't work out well. Folks just think you've done a sloppy ballasting job.

Notice that this yard is laid out on a curve. Railroads prefer to build their yards straight, but sometimes—along rivers and especially in mountains—they have no choice but to curve them.

On model railroads, we often just don't have a wall that's long enough or in the right place, and so have to curve our yards also. It works out a lot better if we can establish some geological feature that makes the bend necessary. Of course, by doing this we're asking for coupling difficulties, but the prototypes have those too.

The tower at Hazard, Ky., is a surprisingly modern affair that looks more like it belongs at an airport. Although not exactly like it, Alpine Division Scale Models' HO scale no. 80 modern yard tower has the right spirit. And, of course, you could always scratchbuild. This tower wouldn't be that difficult.

It's April 1983, and coal from the hills all around Hazard, Ky., is being assembled into trains at the Louisville & Nashville coal-marshalling yard.

Lots of kits are available that you could use to represent those two beat-up sheds. On them, you could exercise your distressing and weathering talents to the fullest. Draw the teeth of a razor saw along a board here and there. Also, try the old peeling-paint trick. Paint the structure gray, dab on patches of rubber cement (don't overdo it), apply the finish paint, then pull off the rubber cement splotches with wadded masking tape.

John Roberts took the lead photo of the Hazard marshalling yard from this unusual suspension foot-

KEY MATERIALS

Tower
Alpine Division Scale Models' HO scale no. 80 modern yard tower

Scenery
Woodland Scenics poly fiber, scenery cement, and ground foam.

John Roberts

Overhead footbridges, like this suspension bridge over the Hazard, Ky., marshalling yard, are another way to break up a yard's linearity.

bridge (right). To the left it goes across the Kentucky River to the town of Hazard. There's a highway and a place to park your car up to the right. If you were actually modeling Hazard, you wouldn't dare leave out this bridge; one like it would also add a lot of interest to a free-lanced coal-hauling railroad.

Appalachian mountain scenery lends itself to modeling with poly fiber balls stretched thin, sprayed with an adhesive, and sprinkled with ground foam. Woodland Scenics makes these materials, which are available in hobby shops. You can also find poly fiber in arts and crafts stores. You wouldn't even want to think about modeling such a forest tree-by-tree.

John Roberts

Often we modelers have to locate a tunnel right at the end of a yard, so it's a little comforting to see a prototype for it. The Louisville & Nashville's main line curves through the tunnel; the tracks to the right are local.

A tunnel like this would be handy for entering a staging yard.

13

RAILROAD YARDS

Hal Miller

Loading pigs

Basic ingredients of an intermodal hub

Today's major city intermodal yards are vast operations that would take up most of our real estate if we tried to model them. On the other hand, if we look to some smaller cities we can find some attainable prototypes, like the Burlington Northern's intermodal hub in Tulsa, Okla. It has all the basic ingredients, but without the duplication we'd find in larger facilities.

First off is a make-up track on the right where flatcars can be loaded and unloaded via the travelling overhead crane. This crane, made by Mi-Jack, is a budget model and is operated from the ground via radio control. For HO, Walthers no. 3122 Mi-Jack Translift, a heavier-duty model, would be just fine. The N scale equivalent is no. 3222.

Trucks drop trailers or containers on the apron and the crane picks them up, shifts them sideways, and places them on flatcars.

The Burlington Northern's intermodal hub in Tulsa, Okla., photographed in 1993.

Unloading is the reverse. Often in both operations the trailers are lined up and waiting.

Highway tractors arriving at the hub enter through the gate at the right of the picture and check in at the office building in the middle of the shot.

When leaving, the trucks check out at the smaller office left of the main one. In front of that smaller office is a "mule," a special tractor with a half cab for better visibility in moving trailers around the grounds.

GHQ has a metal kit for an N scale Ottawa yard tractor. I don't know of one for HO.

Note the trailers in the background behind the office waiting for their next movements.

For a lot more information on modeling an intermodal port, see Jeff Wilson's book *The Model Railroader's Guide to Intermodal Equipment & Operations*, published by Kalmbach Publishing Co.

KEY MATERIALS

Overhead cranes
Walthers nos. 3122 (HO) and 3222 (N) Mi-Jack Translift plastic kits
GHQ Mi-Jack Translift in N, a highly detailed cast-metal and etched-brass model (out of production)

Yard office
Pikestuff's no. 162 or Walthers' no. 3517 yard office (HO)
Pikestuff no. 8017 office building and warehouse (N)

Yard goat
GHQ's Ottawa yard tractor (N)

John Roberts

RAILROAD YARDS

Modeling past and present

An easy-to-build yard office

Every yard needs a yard office. It can be big and impressive, like the yard office we saw at Butler, Wis., or it can be small like this one at the Clinchfield Railroad's interchange yard in Elkhorn City, Ky. It's September 1979 and the Clinchfield is swapping cars with the Chesapeake & Ohio. What's here is certainly interesting, but so is what is not.

Note the old foundation to the right, proof that a building once stood here. You can model such remnants of the past with styrene strips or get fancier and mold them in plaster. Either way it gives your railroad a history. Allen McClelland had all sorts of touches like this on his previous HO Virginia & Ohio, and they contributed to that layout's greatness.

An old foundation will give your yard, or any scene, some history.

As far as modeling the yard office that is there, a very effective material for modeling the siding would be plain old typing paper. You can scribe the lines on the paper with a pencil or a ballpoint pen, using grooved styrene as a guide, then cement the paper to cardboard or sheet styrene with white glue. The glue will cause the paper to swell just a little and give you a crinkled and dinged look that is just right.

Another choice for the siding would be Williams Brothers' no. 60100 crimped siding, made of thin aluminum. Grandt Line plastic windows would work well here and have the delicate mullions you see in the picture.

> **KEY MATERIALS**
>
> **Siding**
> Williams Brothers no. 60100 crimped aluminum siding
> **Windows**
> Grandt Line plastic windows

Junk adds some realism and, even more importantly, color to the scene. And speaking of details, notice that mini-stream that has formed between the shed and the old foundation. Nature never gives up in her attempts to redefine the land.

The hillside beyond the yard forms a natural backdrop for our Clinchfield yard scene.

15

RAILROAD YARDS

Merk Hobson

Caboose for supplies

Convert old equipment into storage sheds

Often railroads converted old equipment to storage or maintenance sheds, and Merk Hobson found this wonderful example at the Chicago & North Western yard in Fond du Lac, Wis. As the lettering indicates, it was used to store caboose supplies and coal. (Cabooses needed coal for their stoves for heating and, depending on the crew's culinary skills and interests, a little cooking.)

The railroad's choice of a caboose for this application makes a lot of sense. The house-type doors at each end make coming and going easy, but they can be locked for security. (Among the supplies stored would be torpedos and flares, equipment you definitely wouldn't want curious kids getting hold of.)

Heaving a boxcar door open every time you needed some supplies would be quite a chore, and old passenger cars would have far too many windows to board over for security's sake.

A model of this caboose turned storage shed in Fond du Lac, Wis., would be colorful and offer you a chance to demonstrate your modeling skills.

You'd think a model like this would be easy, but you'd be wrong. As far as I know, no one makes a plastic HO wood bay-window caboose. In March 2003 Mike Porter's Crummies released a laser-cut wood model for an HO Minneapolis & St. Louis model prototype, which may be hard to find. It was

Merk Hobson

KEY MATERIALS

Mike Porter's Crummies HO Minneapolis & St. Louis laser-cut wood model (distributed by the Chicago & North Western Historical Society, 2053 Partridge Lane, Kalamazoo, MI 49009-3009).

Roundhouse 30-foot wood-sided cupola-type caboose

distributed by the Chicago & North Western Historical Society (see address in Key Materials box). It's a $40 kit, so you might not want to use it as a supply shed. On the other hand, you might. I've found model railroaders will "bear any burden" if they want something badly enough. And of course there's always scratchbuilding, not too tough in this case as your model doesn't have to move.

Another option would be to settle for a wood-sided cupola type (a steel bay window caboose just wouldn't have that funky character). You could remove the cupola and just cover the hole with a patch. That's what a real railroad would do. Card stock would be fine for the job. A Roundhouse 30-footer ought to work well.

Do as the North Western did and paint out the railroad makings. You could use pieces of thin styrene (.010" is .87" in HO) or cardboard to make the plywood panels that are nailed over the window openings. I'd drag a razor saw blade lightly over the material to distress it, then brush-paint it gray with a little black worked in here and there for a weathered look.

Airbrush on the red thinly, letting some of the gray peek through here and there. You could use rub-on letters (dry transfers) or alphabet decals for the lettering, or you could make the lettering on your computer and then make your own decals on a copy machine.

A model like this can be particularly effective on a layout set in modern times. It evokes a sense of the railroad's history and allows you to do some funky modeling you couldn't justify otherwise.

You'd have to use your imagination, but you could have a lot of fun making this model with a removable roof and detailing the interior.

And don't forget the wheelbarrow. Your crew members will find it handy for transporting the coal.

17

ENGINEHOUSES AND TERMINALS

Linn H. Westcott

Keep 'em moving

A simple diesel service facility

Linn Westcott took this set of photos at the Detroit, Toledo & Ironton's engine terminal in June of 1958. In an age when most diesels wore blacks, grays, and dark colors (at least in the east), the DT&I distinguished its locomotives with a bright orange. The DT&I was a well-kept railroad to begin with, but the service equipment here is looking particularly good because it's fairly new. The DT&I wasn't completely dieselized until 1955.

The DT&I is one of those regional lines that sees only a handful of trains a day, so its facilities are rather straightforward and simple, making it a good case study for model railroaders. Certainly *Model Railroader* Magazine senior editor Jim Hediger thinks so; the DT&I has provided the inspiration for his HO scale Ohio Southern for 40 years.

In 1958 the DT&I's through freights terminated at Jackson, while service over the final 51 miles to Ironton (on the Ohio River) was provided by a local freight. Cars were interchanged to the Baltimore & Ohio in Jackson and with the Norfolk & Western at Ironton. All the DT&I engines had to be serviced here before returning northbound over the DT&I's big hill.

The DT&I's diesel service termi-

Engine terminals can be pretty basic, as shown in this photo of the DT&I's diesel service facility at Jackson, Ohio.

nal at Jackson was about as basic and simple as it gets. The sand tower (left) replenishes its supply from the hopper car in the background via a pneumatic system that used compressed air from an engine's air brake system. (Sand hatches on diesels are located atop the hoods at the ends.) Note the grass that has found a toehold here and there in the track ballast. Just a smidge of green ground foam could be used to represent it. Go easy, this can easily be overdone.

This building (right) houses a pump that moves diesel fuel from tanks in the ground to the locomotive fueling columns via those pipes we see. The aboveground tank is for the small gas engine that drives the pump. Williams Bros. pipes and fittings kit (no. 62000) will allow you to build a reasonable representation, as will elbows and pipes from Plastruct.

Any number of the small yard structures available in HO and N scales could serve as your terminal's pumphouse.

Linn H. Westcott

Sand towers from IHC (5005), Stewart Products (102), and Plastruct (1011) would fill the bill here, although you could also scratchbuild one, in which case a Tichy safety cage ladder would add a lot.

Sanding towers add a welcome vertical element to engine terminal scenes and are readily available.

KEY MATERIALS

Fuel pumps
Williams Bros. pipes and fittings kit (no. 62000)
Plastruct elbows and pipes

Sand tower
IHC (5005), Stewart Products (102), and Plastruct (1011)
Tichy safety cage ladder
Hose reel
Styrene and brass shapes

Linn H. Westcott

Right of the lightpost is the hose reel for refueling locomotives. It's not all that different from what you see down at your neighborhood gas station and would be easy to fabricate with bits of styrene and brass shapes. The pole lights keep the engine terminal operating 24 hours a day, and a lighted fueling platform would certainly make a dramatic scene for the modeler who wants day/night operations.

Track end bumpers enliven scenes and you can buy them in kits.

Linn H. Westcott

19

Linn H. Westcott

As the lettering on the car side points out, this car is dedicated especially to sand service. The DT&I had about a dozen such cars which hauled dried sand from a dealer in Michigan to the various DT&I terminals.

You could easily repaint any older-style 2-bay covered hopper and place it in sand service.

This closer-up shot of the fueling rig will help in modeling. Just fake it with bits and pieces.

The fuel pump seen here (left) would be an especially interesting detail to build for a layout. Notice the electrical junction box with on-off buttons and the crank to be attached for rolling up the hose.

The hose reel in the middle of the shot is for the air supply hose. Rust on the wheel tread tells us this sand service car hasn't moved for at least several days.

Linn H. Westcott

John Roberts

Fill 'er up

Butler, Pa., fuel dock

Just for the sake of confusion, we have two Butler yards in this book: one in Wisconsin and this one in western Pennsylvania on the Buffalo & Pittsburgh. (The B&P was spun off from the Chessie System in April 1988, and this photo was taken in October.)

Note the fellows to the right digging a trench, perhaps for an electric or telephone line. At any rate they've gotten the attention of the crewmen standing on the walkway of Baltimore & Ohio no. 4342. The potential for a mini-scene on your layout is obvious. And that little green shed in the middle of the picture is about as "modelgenic" as it gets.

Note also the fuel and sand supply hoses. One problem in discussing these is that although they were available from vendors (you can find pictures of all sorts of them in the various Locomotive Cyclopedias), they were more often homebuilt and vary from one railroad to the next. Only the fellows who worked there know for sure just what all the equipment was for.

The main consideration in modeling engine-service platforms is to account for meeting a locomotive's needs with fuel, sand, water, and lubricants. A good reference is

A motley assortment of motive power had pulled in for service on this bright fall day.

Marty McGuirk's *The Model Railroader's Guide to Locomotive Servicing Terminals* (Kalmbach Publishing Co.).

Note in the background of this photo yet another good prototype for a highway crossing a yard. And note the road coming down and curving under it. This is an old scenery trick that'll get 'em every time. And how about that mud puddle in the foreground?

ENGINEHOUSES AND TERMINALS

ENGINEHOUSES AND TERMINALS

Laying off in Ludlow

A contemporary diesel servicing facility

The enginehouse at Ludlow, Ky., would provide a perfect prototype for a medium-sized model railroad. The building is sheathed with corrugated steel that could be represented with Plastruct no. 91509 styrene sheet or with Campbell HO aluminum siding. For that row of six ventilators running down the roof, you could use Alpine Division Scale Models no. 114 or Cibolo Crossing no. 240. You can elevate either by mounting them on lengths of brass tubing.

The Ludlow engine dock is set up to service several sets of locomotives at a time, and the twin sand towers make a handsome sight standing there like sentinels.

That rig on the left may be a

Here's the three-stall enginehouse at Ludlow, Ky., photographed in September of 1986.

portable steam cleaner. Even if it's not, a steam cleaner would still be a good thing to have around a diesel facility for knocking the mud and dirt off diesel trucks, particularly the brake equipment.

KEY MATERIALS

Enginehouse
Corrugated steel: Plastruct no. 91509 styrene sheet or Campbell HO aluminum siding
Ventilators: Alpine Division Scale Models no. 114 or Cibolo Crossing no. 240
Brass tubing
Sand towers
American Limited no. 5100 sanding towers and no. 5200 fuel cranes
Steam cleaner

Note how the silver sand towers brighten the scene.

John Roberts

The one and only

An enginehouse built solid as a rock

The Winifrede Railroad had only one enginehouse, but that worked out fine because it had only one engine, SW1500 no. 13. The Winifrede began running coal trains in 1882 and interchanged with the Chesapeake & Ohio at Winifrede Jct., some 7 miles away, although most of the WRR coal was delivered to a barge-loading terminal. The WRR owned a surprisingly large fleet of hopper cars (200), many of them ancient and not allowable in interchange service.

This solid old enginehouse is built of concrete block that you could represent quite well in HO with Rix no. 1004 block wall panels. The doors are made of corrugated steel sheet, which you could model with Campbell aluminum siding cut into individual sheets glued on cardboard, or you could use Evergreen's styrene corrugated siding. The bracing could be Evergreen or Plastruct angle. Evidently this is a sliding door, as there appears to be a door track atop the door to the left.

About halfway down the side wall you can see brick construction with windows. Beyond that you see some stone construction. There's a ventilator on top of the building, and you'd probably want to add several so your workers won't be overcome by fumes. A Cibolo Crossing no. 19 slatted vent kit would be in character.

The diesel fuel pump to the right looks just like the one you would have seen down at the corner filling station about 30 years ago. An SS Ltd. no. 2453 gas pump would look great here.

The sign says, "Danger, close clearance," a warning to brakemen who might be riding the sides of cars.

The Winifrede Railroad enginehouse at West Carbon near Charleston, W. Va., in August, 1983.

KEY MATERIALS

Enginehouse
Concrete block: Rix no. 1004 block wall panels (HO)
Doors: Campbell aluminum siding cut into individual sheets glued on cardboard or Evergreen styrene corrugated siding
Bracing: Evergreen or Plastruct angle
Ventilator: Cibolo Crossing no. 19 slatted vent kit

Diesel fuel pump
SS Ltd. no. 2453 gas pump

ENGINEHOUSES AND TERMINALS

Merk Hobson

Small, yet significant

A pocket-sized enginehouse

If there was ever a small engine facility that cried out to be modeled, this is it. You could find room for it on even the smallest of layouts. That switcher's duties must have been pretty important to the railroad, or more likely a customer, as it's unusual to see such lavish quarters for one engine.

Milwaukee Road switch engine no. 630, an SW1200, fits neatly in its house with only about 6 feet on either side to spare. For HO scale, the Pikestuff no. 5000 single-stall enginehouse would do well, built straight out of the box, and it's even blue with white trim, so you wouldn't have to paint it. If you wanted to make it closer to the prototype, you'd need to reduce the height and width. Pikestuff offers the same structure in N (no. 8002).

I'm not sure what that tank on the side is for, but it would be easy to represent. Kibri offers an HO industrial accessories set (no. 8103)

It's 1967 and we're in Seattle. You won't find an enginehouse much smaller than this.

that would yield an appropriate tank and a lot of other details and piping you could use here and

KEY MATERIALS	
Single-stall enginehouse Pikestuff no. 5000 in HO, no. 8002 in N	Hoses: small-diameter insulated electrical wire Black fuel tank: HO Kibri no. 948
Tank Kibri HO industrial accessories set (no. 8103)—tank, details, and piping Kibri N scale set (no. 6690) Sanding rig: brass rod or tubing	Concrete containment wall: sheet styrene (HO, 060" thick; N, 040") **Turntable** Walthers 90-foot kit Micro-Engineering, Atlas, or Central Valley girders Athearn SW1500 cab no. 39001 (HO)

Tapered girders make this turntable bridge most unusual.

there on your layout. Kibri has a similar set (no. 6690) for N scale.

The sanding rig would be an easy project, using brass rod or tubing. Small-diameter insulated electrical wire works well for hoses.

The sand spills on the track will cost you only a few pinches of light-colored dirt from your lawn or driveway, or you can buy a bag of material at the hobby shop.

On the rear of the enginehouse we spot an all-weather entrance and a black fuel tank with its own containment wall so that if the tank ruptures the oil won't get far. In HO a Kibri no. 948 tank would be perfect.

You could make the concrete containment wall from sheet styrene. It should be 6" to 8" thick, which for HO would work out to about .060" thick, .040" for N.

That turntable is quite unusual. You might start with a Walthers 90-foot turntable kit and scratch-

Merk Hobson

build the unusual sides or try kitbashing them from Micro Engineering, Atlas, or Central Valley girders.

The pit wall is lined with timbers (perhaps railroad ties). The turntable is unusual in that there's no escape track at the end nearest the camera. The engine just runs onto the bridge, is turned 180 degrees, and runs off again.

Note the grass, weeds, and debris on the pit bottom. Larger and busier turntables had concrete-lined pit floors with a drainage system to prevent standing water.

The turntable in this photo is not the same Milwaukee Road turntable we've been discussing, but I just had to get this shot in this book somewhere. What do you do if you're the yardmaster and the decades-old wooden control shack on your turntable has come to the end of the road? Here it looks like some creative type kitbashed a new shed by using parts from the cab off a switch engine. Note the all-weather window.

If you'd like to add such a cab to your turntable, a good starting point

in HO scale would be an Athearn SW1500 cab. These are sold separately as part no. 39001. But be forewarned: in the minds of many modelers, a little of this sort of rather fanciful thing goes a long way.

The sign on the cab says "All blocks must be in place on all unattended locomotives," and there's a good reason for that rule. Nothing makes quite as embarrassing a mess as a locomotive that has crept into the turntable pit. Not only is it rough on the locomotive—and the hostler!—but when that happens, those engines in the roundhouse are trapped until the "big hook" comes in and cleans up.

On Nov. 9, 1983, the Milwaukee Road chose its hometown to introduce its "running Indian" paint scheme to the railroad press.

George Drury

25

ENGINEHOUSES AND TERMINALS

Jim Hediger

Shelter without substance

C&IM's single-stall enginehouse

This spartan single-stall enginehouse on the Chicago & Illinois Midland Railroad in Taylorville, Ill., is about as plunk in the middle of the state as you can get. The C&IM is a coal hauler running from a port on the Illinois River at Havana some 80 miles to a giant power plant at Taylorville, about 25 miles southeast of Springfield. It's one of the best-maintained railroads you'll see anywhere.

This very simple structure is probably of pole construction (wood poles anchored in the ground with horizontal planks spaced every four feet or so to tie the poles together). The building is sheathed with corrugated sheet steel. One simple way to model it would be to use Campbell's corrugated aluminum sheeting cut into individual panels and mounted with Walthers Goo on cardboard

Chicago & Illinois Midland Railroad single-stall enginehouse in Taylorville, Ill., photographed on November 3, 1985.

walls. This would work equally well for both HO and N scales.

Note the corner strips. These could be made from heavy paper. If you've built any of Campbell's sheet-metal kits, you'll have no problems. This is a labor-intensive

Jim Hediger

method but would be well worthwhile here because there are only simple shapes and no doors and windows to work around. This material has an advantage over plastic sheet in that little dents and dings that occur while modeling appear quite natural.

The aluminum does not take paint well, but you'll get acceptable results if you first spray the building with Testors Dull Cote to give the surface some "tooth." A flat gray yields the look of galvanized steel, and a little drybrushing with Boxcar Red and Tuscan will add some neat rusting effects.

The little green shed would make a fascinating model in its own right. Paint it gray and lightly drybrush on some green here and there. The fueling pump and other vitals couldn't be much simpler.

Maybe it's my imagination, but it looks like an old Coke machine is being used as a protective cover.

The photo of the rear of the engine shed shows C&IM no. 22, an SW1200, lurking inside. The most interesting features here are junction boxes and the piping that houses the electric wires.

Note the simple track bumper, just two ties anchored in the ground. If the engine gets a little frisky and takes these out, replacing them is a simple and inexpensive proposition. Concrete or steel bumpers can get to be a significant investment.

The old concrete slab suggests that a more substantial building may once have stood here.

You could build the Taylorville enginehouse from plastic sheet in a few hours.

KEY MATERIALS

Enginehouse

Campbell's corrugated aluminum sheeting
Cardboard
Walthers Goo
Heavy paper
Testors Dull Cote
Boxcar Red paint
Tuscan Red paint

ENGINEHOUSES AND TERMINALS

John Roberts

Down and dirty

A steel-sheathed enginehouse in decline

If you're modeling a remote short line that's often strapped for cash, then this enginehouse might be for you. It's located at Palmerton, Pa., and serves the Chestnut Ridge Railway.

If you haven't heard of the Chestnut Ridge, you have lots of company. It's a 7.2-mile-long line that runs from Palmerton to a connection with Conrail at Little Gap, Pa. As of 1986 it owned one locomotive, an Alco S-2 switcher,

although it also operated locomotives owned by and lettered for the New Jersey Zinc Co., which owns the Chestnut Ridge. (There's a zinc mine at Palmerton.)

This is yet another railroad building sheathed with galvanized steel, which was so widely used from the 1920s until the 1960s or so, when prefabricated steel buildings (such as those made by Butler) became the norm.

Again, you can use Campbell's corrugated aluminum or plastic material from Evergreen or Plastruct. You can even make your own siding by scribing bond paper with a ball-point pen, using scribed styrene or wood as a guide. Model railroad author E.L. Moore used this method with great results. He always preferred a dried-out pen,

Chestnut Ridge Railway enginehouse in Palmerton, Pa. John Roberts took this photograph in July 1984.

though, probably just because he wanted to make sure he'd gotten all the writing out of it he could.

The wood doors show the effects of wind, rain, and time. The one on the left has been repaired (not very successfully) by nailing on some siding material.

The right-of-way is no better than it has to be, and you can get this look by sprinkling a little scenic ground foam on your ballast. I wouldn't try it when you're bonding ballast and everything is wet because you wouldn't have enough control over where the weeds are going.

KEY MATERIALS

Enginehouse
Campbell's corrugated aluminum or Evergreen's or Plastruct's plastic
Ground foam
Woodland Scenics scenery cement

Those doors are a funk modelers dream come true.

On dry ballast you can get the weeds just where you want them. If I have too many or some in places where I don't want them, I just sneak up on them with a vacuum cleaner hose. It's surprising how well this works to remove the foam you want to while leaving the rest behind. Anchor the foliage you want with a little adhesive applied with an eyedropper. Woodland Scenics scenery cement is excellent for this.

The Chestnut Ridge turntable (photo below) is in a class all by itself, but the basic ingredients are there: a pit complete with a pit wall, a bridge pivoted in the middle so it can turn, a ring rail, and wheels at each end of the bridge to support it while it's turning. Notice on the mainline track to the right that, viewed from this angle, we can see no ballast at all.

A model of the turntable at Chestnut Ridge would add lots of character to a short line scene.

John Roberts

John Roberts

BRIDGES

Arches and flyovers
Spanning the Susquehanna

Thumbing through a stack of black-and-white photos, I pause at a beautiful study of a steam train crossing a stone arch bridge in silhouette against a glistening broad river. I've been transported to the west bank of the Susquehanna River just a mile or so north of the Pennsylvania Railroad's renowned Enola Yard, and I'm looking at the Rockville Bridge.

"Get real," my practical side is saying. "No one has the space to model that." But the adventurous side is saying, "Not so fast. Someone might want to run it along an entire wall or down the middle of a basement. Or it might be just the ticket for taking a railroad across a door and into hidden staging. And you could always compress it."

The Rockville Bridge, as shown in the photo above, is an impressive sight indeed. The bridge's 48

F. L. Jaques

arches were built in sets of eight with double-wide piers connecting them. This eased construction by breaking the project into what amounted to six end-to-end bridges and also assured that the entire bridge wouldn't go down like a row of dominoes if an arch should somehow be destroyed.

On both sides of the Susquehanna River, the Pennsylvania Railroad encountered high ridges and so had to swing the tracks north and south. We model railroaders often encounter the same problem, although for us the obstacle is usually a basement wall, not a mountain. A bluff or ridge blocking our way will justify a curve.

Other photos showed how interesting the track arrangements were at each end of the bridge. The bridge supported four mainline tracks that swept off north and south at each end, in the process crossing over and connecting with the tracks that ran parallel with the river. It was like a modern interstate highway interchange, and for modelers looking to run lots of trains, the possibilities are enormous.

The Rockville Bridge near Harrisburg, Pa., in 1952, is an inspiring sight.

A little history

Today's Rockville Bridge is the third one the PRR built at this site. The first, finished in 1849, was a series of twenty-three 140-foot wood deck trusses reinforced on each side with a sweeping wooden arch and supported by stone piers. There was one track.

The second bridge, completed in 1877, was also a deck type, but this time the trusses were built of iron

31

Frank Spieles

By July of 1987, the Rockville Bridge had been inherited by Conrail.

and sized to fit on the original bridge's piers. Over the years, trains had become longer and heavier and traffic had grown steadily, so the new bridge supported two tracks.

The present bridge was built slightly south of the two earlier bridges on new piers. Consisting of forty-eight 70-foot stone arches, it has often been called the world's longest stone-arch railroad bridge, which isn't exactly true. The wall and arch surfaces are indeed stone several feet thick, but the inside was filled with concrete. For a complete and highly readable book, complete with photos of all three Rockville bridges and their construction, get Dan Cupper's *Rockville Bridge: Rails Across the Susquehanna* (Withers Publishing, 2002).

Over its 100 years, the bridge has hosted with distinction four railroad companies: the Pennsylvania, the Penn Central, Conrail, and Norfolk Southern. The one black mark against its record came on August 19, 1997, when the wall above one arch collapsed and put four loaded CSX coal hoppers into the river. The wall was repaired with cast concrete made to look like the original stonework.

Modeling the bridge

Model Railroad Stoneworks specializes in PRR and Erie cast-plaster arch bridges and has kits for the Rockville Bridge and for the Erie's famous Starrucca Viaduct. You can check them out at modelrailroadstoneworks.com or call 215-321-1331.

Probably the best choice for a similar bridge using HO plastic kits would be Kibri's no. 9640, which gives you a single-track, three-arch bridge that is 13¾" long. This is a beautifully molded kit that has built-in provision for being combined with more kits to make a longer and wider bridge. You can make the bridge taller using pier set no. 9646.

One obvious drawback would be cost. A single bridge kit is $23.99, so an imposing structure would very quickly get up into the hundreds of dollars. Nor would it be as imposing as the real Rockville Bridge in that the arches would be only about half as wide.

N scalers have a good option with the Atlas no. 2826. You get a four-arch bridge for only $4.15, so for less than 50 bucks you could put together something pretty impressive, although the arches would still be smallish. I'd cut the piers off shorter to bring the proportions more in line with those of the Rockville Bridge. Those tall piers, incidentally, make this an excellent kit for a viaduct crossing a fairly deep canyon.

Rolling your own Rockville Bridge

For the Rockville Bridge, I would use homemade plaster castings, and if I wanted to compress it (and I almost certainly would), I would make the arches scale size

D. R. Jacobson

Those islands are the remains of earlier bridge piers.

but just use fewer of them. The drawings and photos here should get you started.

First, I'd make a plain master (no stone detail) about ½" thick from wood or styrene. I'd make a rubber mold of that, make a plaster casting, then carve in the stone detail, using a straightedge and hobby knife. This carved casting would become the pattern for a final rubber mold for casting as many copies as I needed.

Micro-Mark is one source for RTV rubber and other casting materials you would need. Packaged with those products come more-detailed suggestions for making mold boxes, using a release agent, and other tricks of the casting trade.

Depending on how prototypical you want to get, and whether your

This through-girder bridge would make a good modeling project in its own right.

bridge would be viewable from both sides, you may need two arch molds, one for the upriver and another for the downriver sides of the bridge. The upriver side has a pointed cutwater, typical of stone or concrete piers, that deflects the current down each side of the pier with minimal erosion and less debris or ice piling up.

The bridge was made of sandstone, mostly from western Pennsylvania, and when new it was a soft brown color. Over the years it's picked up natural black "varnish" that makes it look drybrushed by nature.

The top of the bridge was coated with asphalt, then a layer of cinders was applied before the track ballast went on. Applying such a base coat of cinders to roadbed was a practice seen commonly, especially in the east, until the steam era ended and cinders became a rarity on the railroad.

Philip R. Hastings

33

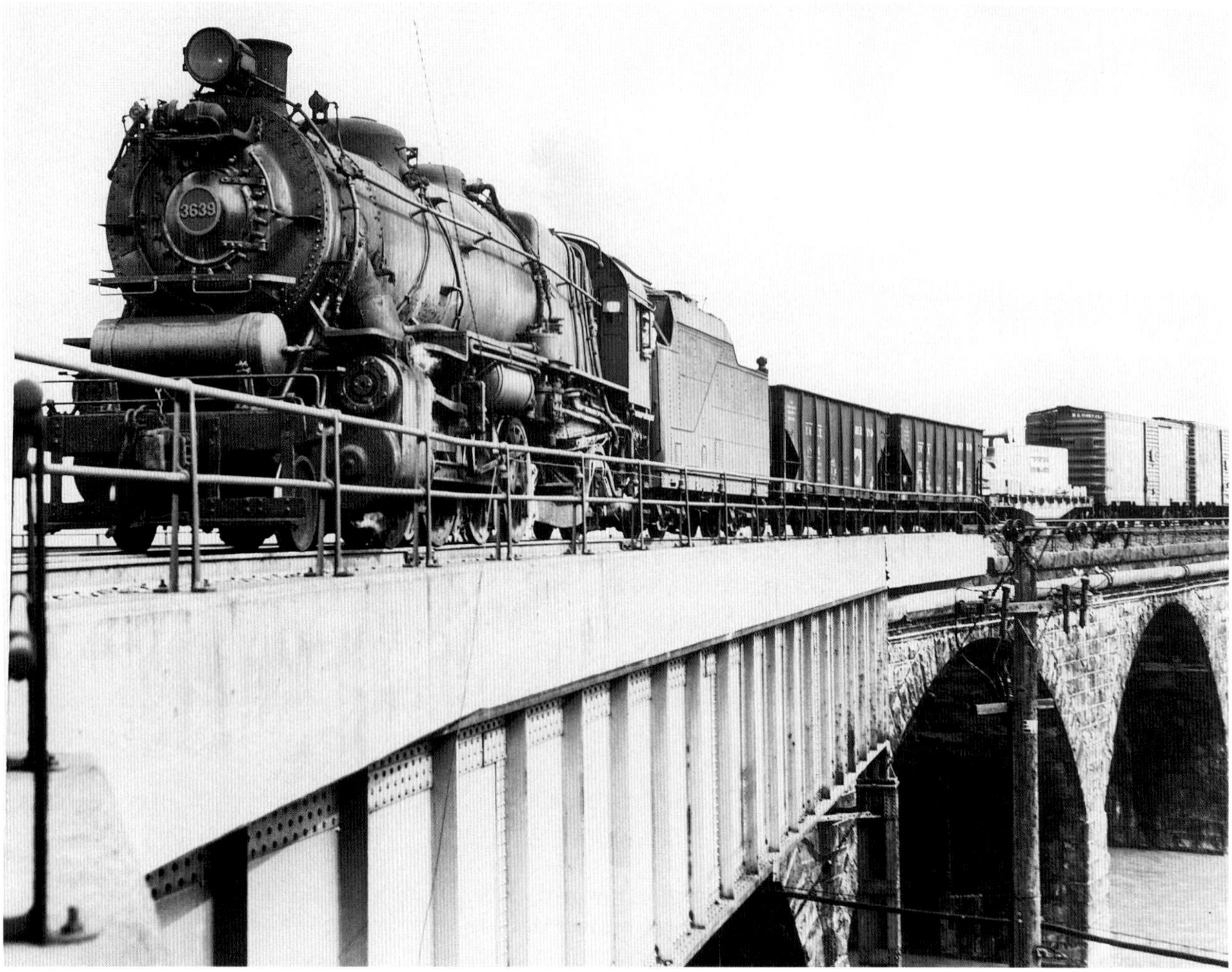

Don Wood

This girder was needed to accommodate a broader curve than the original bridge plans had called for.

Squeezing so much track between the bluffs and river called for lots of cutting and filling.

Linn H. Westcott

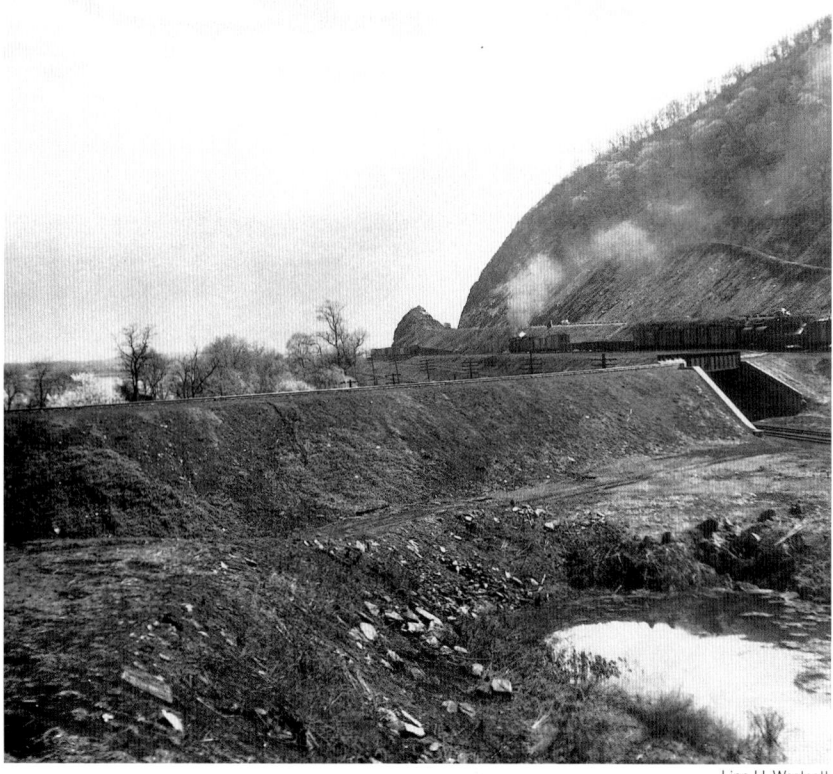

The Pennsy promoted its 4-track mainline as its "Broadway."

You'll often see cinders on the sides of fills and embankments; they add a realistic (and often missing) modeling touch.

The autumn 1952 photo (page 33, bottom) shows two of the spans that carry trains coming off the Rockville Bridge and above lines running along the river. The span in the foreground is a through-girder type. In HO a Micro Engineering no. 75520 50-foot bridge would work well to represent it.

If your tracks cross at a shallower angle, you might need a longer bridge, in which case Central Valley's no. 1903, a 72-footer, would be good and is also highly detailed. It's easy to modify the length of girders. Just be careful about making them too long, as they won't look right. If a girder's depth isn't proportional to its length, it won't be sufficiently strong.

Atlas' no. 885 HO one-piece bridge (no. 2548 in N scale) is ready to be plugged into the layout, but is less prototypical in that there's insufficient support structure under the track. An easy fix is to cut the girders off and glue them to the sides of your roadbed for a ballasted deck bridge. You can do the same with Micro Engineering girders, which are sold separately.

Note, in the Hastings photo on page 33, the signal head mounted in the middle of the bridge girder. This would be an easy detail. You could cut the head off an inexpensive plastic signal or choose to make something more elaborate and wired. Your signal department would save lots of money on installation plus have a signal that's easy to get to for maintenance.

The silver bridge further back and left would be a simple matter of cementing a girder to roadbed. Steel bridges, if they're painted at all, are almost always painted black or silver; very occasionally you'll see a dark green. More recent bridges, made with better steel, oxidize to a pleasing soft brown color, and since the oxidized surface inhibits further rusting, they are left unpainted.

The larger photo on page 34 gives us a closer look at the silver bridge girder shown in the

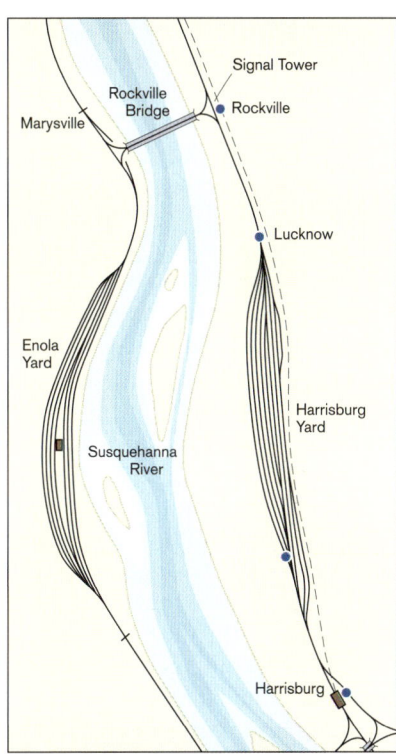

Westbound PRR passenger trains usually crossed the Susquehanna south of Harrisburg. Freights used the Rockville Bridge.

When and where to model stone arch bridges

Arch bridges are a beautiful sight, whether a single short span crossing a stream or a majestic series of arches marching across a valley. Despite their mass, they look light and airy. They seem to complement nature rather than overwhelm it. Here are some thoughts on modeling stone arch bridges that will look as if they belong.

Time period: Most stone arch bridges in the United States were built in the late 1800s and early 1900s during a time when the major railroads were growing rapidly and making lots of money. Railroad bridges have to carry extremely heavy loads and, in an age when far less was known about designing and building steel bridges than now, stone arch bridges were much simpler and totally reliable. After all, the Romans had pretty much worked the engineering out and proved that such structures were good for several thousand years and counting.

Stone arch bridges were expensive to build, but the railroads had the money and were willing to part with it. In fact, they had no choice if they were to meet the escalating demand for their services and keep up with the competition.

Beyond such economic considerations, these works doubled as monuments to the railroad's power and influence. Building the stone bridges required skilled labor, but such men were available for low wages. (Most of the stonecutters were Italian immigrants.)

As you cross the country from east to west you see fewer stone railroad structures. This was certainly not due to a lack of rocks, but because, at the turn of the century, the western railroads were still young and had not achieved the traffic density found in the east. By the time they did, steel and concrete technology had taken over.

Type of railroad: Your railroad needs to run lots of trains to justify the expense of building such bridges, but once they're built you'll enjoy the economies of low maintenance costs. And you don't have to worry about them burning down, being swept away in a storm, or requiring paint.

Geographical considerations: Stone arches can span nothing like the distances that steel truss bridges can, so lots of piers are required. That means you wouldn't find one on a commercially navigable river where boat or barge traffic would be all too often smacking up against the piers.

Hastings photo. The Pennsy L-1 2-8-2 is pulling 110 cars into Enola Yard in March of 1955. This area owes its cobbled-up appearance to the fact that it was grafted onto the bridge in 1939 to accommodate a track swinging south and directly into Enola Yard. As originally built, the bridge allowed for such a provision but, by the time the PRR got around to it, equipment had grown longer and the railroad needed to swing a bigger curve than had been planned originally.

Unless you're one of the rare exceptions among layout planners and builders, you've probably found yourself in a similar situation where your plans fell short. Why not do as prototype railroads often did? Instead of tearing out an entire area and starting over, figure out a fix that may not look as nice but will cost your engineering department a whole lot less—and be all the more realistic for it.

Oh yes, the river

What's a bridge without a river? To model the river, I'd use a plywood base and coat it with a thin layer of joint compound to hide the grain. After painting the surface a dark blue, almost black, I'd add the rocks, representing them with flat, thin real rocks, or by pouring plaster on wax paper and breaking off suitably sized chunks. A little ground foam could represent the foliage atop the larger rocks that look like baby islands.

Next would come a thin layer of Enviro-Tex. This is a two-part epoxy, found in hardware or home-supply stores, that is easy to use.

Fig. 2 PIER MASONRY

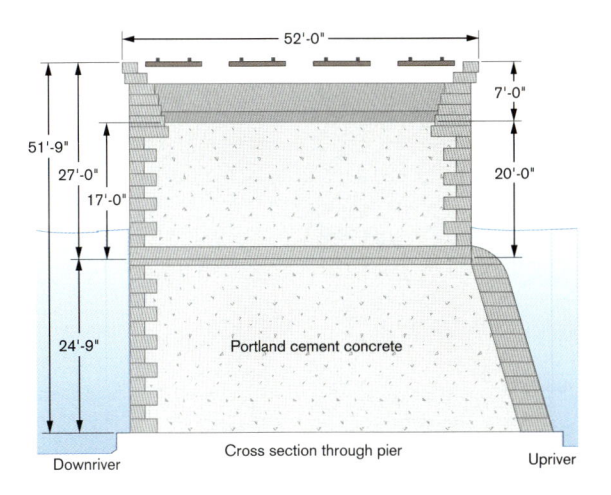

Fig. 2 ARCHES AND ABUTMENT

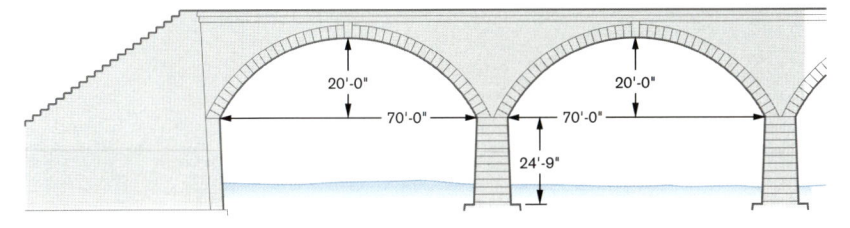

You just mix together equal amounts of the two syrupy liquids and pour. Enviro-Tex does not have an odor that will drive you out of the house like clear casting resin will. Maybe it's just my imagination, but all I can detect is a faint whiff of peanut butter.

The substantial frame houses on the west side of the river, seen in the color photo on page 33, could be represented by kits. Bachmann's Sears Catalog house, offered in both HO and N, has been out of production for a few years but would be a natural if you run across one. (Funaro & Camerlengo offers a cast-epoxy-kit version in HO.)

Other good choices in HO would be the Walthers Cornerstone no. 3601 Aunt Lucy's house and the Atlas Kate's colonial home (available as kit no. 711, or built-up no. 611.) This house is now also available in N. Several of the Craftsman laser-cut wood kits available in both HO and N would also work well, as a perusal of a Walthers Catalog will show.

KEY MATERIALS

Arch bridge kits
Model Railroad Stoneworks: cast plaster (HO)
Kibri no. 9640 single-track, three-arch bridge and pier set no. 9646 (HO)
Atlas no. N 2826 (N)

Scratchbuilding materials
Micro-Mark RTV rubber and other casting materials

Through girder bridge
Micro Engineering no. 75520 50-foot bridge (HO)
Central Valley no. 1903 72-foot bridge (HO)
Atlas no. 885 one-piece bridge (HO) or no. 2548 (N)
Micro Engineering girders

Structures
Bachmann's Sears Catalog house (HO and N)
Funaro & Camerlengo cast-epoxy-kit Sears Catalog house (HO)
Walthers Cornerstone no. 3601 Aunt Lucy's house
Atlas Kate's colonial home (available as kit no. 711, or built-up no. 611), available in both HO and N
Craftsman laser-cut wood kits available in both HO and N

River
Joint compound
Real rocks
Enviro-Tex two-part epoxy

BRIDGES

Flying high

Cascade bridge features towering steel trestles

Here are a couple "high" drama shots taken from a helicopter in the spring of 1983. The subject is the Cascade Bridge at Springville, N.Y., and the photos show us about all we need to know about high steel trestles.

The bridge soars 190 feet above Cattaraugus Creek, is 780 feet long, and was built in 1897 for the Buffalo, Rochester & Pittsburgh Railroad. Later that line became part of the Baltimore & Ohio, which by the time of Mr. Furminger's high-flying photographic adventure had become part of the Chessie System. Today it's part of the Buffalo & Pittsburgh Railroad.

Cascade Bridge at Springville, N.Y., is a classic steel trestle.

It may come as a surprise that this thoroughly modern-looking bridge was actually built five years before the stone arch Rockville Bridge we looked at in the previous section. Obviously terrain dictates design and materials. This bridge had to be high, the stream it crossed was not particularly potent, and the rock walls provided plenty of firm support for the piers.

Years ago I built a similar bridge for Kalmbach Publishing's HO club railroad, the Milwaukee, Racine & Troy, using Micro Engineering's no. 75514 trestle kit. I found these kits are highly "bash-able" (we'll get to that in the next section) and would provide the ingredients for just about any bridge of this basic type you want to represent. Plus, this bridge is also available in N scale (no. 75518).

In real life, we're usually looking up at tall bridges, whereas on our layouts we're often looking down at them, so these two photos offer a big advantage for the model railroader—a bird's-eye view at details we'd like to know about but seldom get to see.

Note in the photos how brush has snagged and piled up on the upstream side of the piers. Doesn't that water look just like a modeler had poured it with Enviro-Tex?

KEY MATERIALS

Deck bridges
Micro Engineering 30- and 50-foot lengths

Towers
Micro Engineering no. 555714 tall steel viaduct kits
Evergreen styrene strips

Piers
RTV rubber mold castings
Hydrocal plaster

Track
Micro Engineering's bridge track
Walthers Goo

The outside wall of a riverbend is typically cut deeper than the inside.

And what a nice job this shows of feathering the bottom color out from the shore.

The top of each tower supports a deck girder bridge, just as with Micro Engineering's kit. Note also that the longer deck girder bridge between towers is also deeper to give it added strength. The longer the span, the deeper the girder needs to be.

The deck trusses would be easy to represent in HO using Atlas's no. 884 deck truss bridge. You could cut off the sides and kitbash them closer together if you wanted multiple trusses as seen here. (I count four.)

Mr. Furminger must have had some special arrangement with the railroad, as the train sat still for him while the helicopter circled around to shoot the bridge from the other side. Cattaraugus Creek isn't very big, but it's done a fair share of rock carving over the eons. A sandbar like that would add interest to any river or stream on your layout. They are found in places where a stream widens, the current slows, and some of the silt being transported drops out.

BRIDGES

Bill Zuback

High up on the MR&T

Kitbashing a high steel trestle

The high trestle shown here is officially named the Gordon Odegard Bridge for our longtime friend and associate editor for *Model Railroader* Magazine. Scenically and literally it's the high point on the Milwaukee, Racine & Troy, Kalmbach Publishing Co.'s HO club railroad.

The first step in building the bridge was figuring out what deck bridges we would need and where they would go, then building them at the workbench. Micro Engineering offers the bridges in both 30- and 50-foot lengths. Keep in mind that between the towers you can also use bridges by other manufacturers, and you can use other bridge types, including through girder and through truss, depending on how long your spans need to be.

We kitbashed the towers from several Micro Engineering no. 555714 tall steel viaduct kits. Gordon Odegard made the piers for our MR&T bridges by first making a master from sheet styrene. Then he made an RTV rubber mold and cast the piers in Hydrocal plaster.

Back when we had built the benchwork, we'd continued the track right through the bridge area so we wouldn't have to wait to run trains. The curve, then, already

Here's the Gordon Odegard bridge on *Model Railroader* Magazine's Milwaukee, Racine & Troy club layout.

Note how the bridge towers were supported on wooden risers prior to scenery being added.

KEY MATERIALS

Trestle
Micro Engineering 30- and 50-foot bridge kits (HO)

Deck truss bridge
Central Valley no. 1902 bridge (HO)
Faller no. 560 bridge (HO)
Kibri no. 7630 (N)

existed, so we made a paper tracing of it by drawing a pencil along the rail edges (like making a rubbing of a coin).

Taking our paper pattern to the workbench, we used it as a guide to bend Micro Engineering's bridge track to the curve. Then we cemented the deck bridges to the underside of the ties with Walthers Goo.

40

Kurt Heiden

Looking west

More high trestles

Despite our previous example, the Cascade Bridge in New York State, we usually associate high steel trestles with western railroading, mainly because in the west the terrain is more rugged and difficult to contend with.

Here's a particularly impressive high steel trestle, this one on the Burlington Northern line at East Glacier Park, Montana. The train is westbound. This bridge, too, could be represented with Micro Engineering bridge kits. Note the extra vertical legs on the faces of each tower for additional support. This bridge is also seen on page 60 where you get a good look at it from the side and get some ideas on how to model the scenery. Note the use of a deck truss bridge to support a wide span. Central

The Burlington Northern's high steel trestle spans Two Medicine Creek at East Glacier Park, Mont.

Valley's no. 1902 bridge would fill the bill here, as would Faller no. 560. In N scale, Kibri's no. 7630 would be a good choice.

Of course, when you mention tall steel trestles, railfans will automatically think of the Western Pacific's northern California route through the Feather River Canyon. Here's one of the line's bridges photographed in 1990 after the Union Pacific had taken over the WP. Looks like all you'd have to do in HO is alternate Micro Engineering's 30- and 50-foot bridges and you'd have it. The WP's silver bridges sure look striking against all those pine trees.

Jim Kelly

The Union Pacific (formerly Western Pacific) trestle in the Feather River Canyon in 1990 is stunning against a backdrop of pines.

BRIDGES

41

BRIDGES

Reid McNaught

They're everywhere

Deck girder bridges

Probably the majority of railroad bridges are simple deck girder types. The differences, and much of the interest, lie in how those girders are supported. The bridge in the photo above (October 1987) is one of eight similar bridges that cross Abo Canyon in northern New Mexico on the Santa Fe's Belen Cutoff. The massive concrete piers feature cutwaters, even though the Abo River is dry most of the time. When rains do come, though, they come hard and there's not much vegetation in these hills to drink up the water. Flash floods can put those piers to the test in a hurry. On the right you can clearly make out the fill that the railroad used to get the tracks out to the abutment.

This Santa Fe bridge is one of eight similar bridges that cross Abo Canyon in northern New Mexico.

This photo of the Southern Pacific's Fifth Crossing of Tehachapi Creek—shot in September 1993—illustrates an important point: a steel bridge's structure needs to be straight, even if the track on it curves. The center girder is longer, and therefore deeper, than the other two.

The loose rail to the right has nothing to do with the bridge. Rail is constantly being replaced on the Tehachapi Pass route and you see lots of it distributed along the right-of-way waiting its turn.

Southern Pacific's Fifth Crossing of Tehachapi Creek could provide a picturesque scene for your layout.

Jim Kelly

Bruce C. Nelson

This 1985 shot on the Chicago & North Western in Marinette, Wis., shows an interesting mix of taller stone and shorter concrete piers. It may be that the stone piers once stood alone and supported through-truss bridges.

This photo reminds us that most long bridges are really a series of short ones.

43

BRIDGES

Charles Streetman

Whatever is is right

Combination bridges

Here we see a Burlington Northern shippers' special crossing the Fox River in Sheridan, Ill., on a bridge that demonstrates the variety of materials and design principles that can go into the design of a single bridge. On the left is a wood timber trestle. Although timber trestles fell out of favor for heavy-use mainline bridges almost a hundred years ago, you'll often see them used for approach spans, as here. Next comes a steel bent on a stone pier that I'd bet was built to accompany an earlier (and lower) bridge.

Next comes a pair of unusual steel bents capped with concrete. The spans appear to be steel I beams. On the right-hand side we find another old stone pier and the beginnings of yet some other bridge type that we can't see enough of to identify. The point is that railroads build bridges first and foremost to keep trains up in the air, and you can mix and match bridge types as long as they make engineering sense. The more you look at real railroads and photos, the better understanding you'll have of what will work and look plausible.

The Chesapeake & Ohio bridge at Madison, W. Va., demonstrates a critical principal of bridge building. Here's another example of old piers being incorporated into a replacement bridge.

And speaking of real railroad practice, the photo in the lower left demonstrates one of the main principles of bridge building. The track on a bridge can be curved, but the bridge structure itself needs to be straight. Oftentimes on a model railroad that means building a series of short bridges to accommodate our curves. Each bridge segment has to be supported at its ends. John Roberts took this shot on the Chesapeake & Ohio at Madison, W. Va., in September 1987.

John Roberts

44

J. David Ingles

Crossing with a twist

East Dubuque's irontruss and swing bridges

At Dubuque, Iowa, the Canadian National's Illinois Central crosses the Mississippi River on a series of classic iron truss bridges with a swing bridge on the Illinois side. When the bridge opened January 1, 1869, the IC was already operating across Iowa, but most of the year they had to depend on ferry boats to transport cars across the river. (In the winter the railroad laid temporary tracks on the ice.)

Andrew Carnegie's Keystone Bridge Co. won the contract for the bridge after he convinced the bridge company's directors that the wrought iron he intended to use extensively was superior to the cast iron proposed by a rival bidder. "A little more money and . . . your bridge would stand against any steamboat. We have never built and we will never build a cheap bridge. Ours don't fall."

So far Carnegie has been right.

And making this area even more dramatic, heading east the IC track no sooner comes off the bridge on the Illinois side than it crosses the Burlington Northern Santa Fe's busy double-track main line and disappears into a tunnel penetrating the high bluff.

Once inside the hill, the line curves hard right to exit and connect with those tracks it just crossed, as if some model railroader had thought it up. (See the map on page 50.)

Built the same year the first transcontinental railroad was completed, the Dubuque bridge has lasted 130 years.

The photo above, taken in September 2002, catches the Illinois Central's daily through-freight from Iowa to Chicago, no. 338, as it crosses the Mississippi from Dubuque, Iowa, to East Dubuque, Ill. To the right is the swing span that pivots 90 degrees to accommodate boat and barge traffic. (The Canadian National now owns the Illinois Central, accounting for the gray paint and "wet noodle" heralds seen here.)

Dave Ingles took this shot in July of 1961 from the Illinois side of the river as a Burlington steam excursion train with 2-8-2 no. 4960 approaches the swing bridge. Note the cutwater on the upstream side of the bridge pier. Steel towers atop each end of the through truss bridges carry electric lines across the river, providing the power to turn the bridge in the process. The bridge tender's house is on the right.

It's July of 1961 as a Burlington steam excursion train with 2-8-2 no. 4960 approaches the swing bridge.

J. David Ingles

An Illinois Central freight exits the bridge on October 30, 1986. The Keystone builder's plate can be seen on the end member to the right. Left, on the far bank, is the Dubuque Star Brewery.

Both Walthers and Central Valley offer single-track through truss bridges in plastic kits. The Walthers kit would be easier to build but has a straight top line. The Central Valley kit does too, but would be easier to kitbash if you wanted a peaked top chord as seen on the prototype bridges at Dubuque.

Thomas Hoffman

It's September of 1987 as a westbound Chicago, Central & Pacific freight emerges from the tunnel at East Dubuque, Ill. Within seconds it will be crossing the Burlington Northern's double-track main line. No tunnel portal was necessary here because the rock was strong and stable and didn't need the support. Basically a tunnel portal is a retaining wall with a hole in it. It doesn't support anything above it, but it prevents the mouth of the tunnel from collapsing outwards.

We can see an edge of the tunnel's concrete liner, however, making this a most interesting candidate for modeling. I would make the liner first, using walls made from thick styrene sheet (.080") or ¼" foam board. Add a plain sheet styrene face and let the cement set thoroughly.

The tunnel liner doesn't need a top unless the viewer can get low enough to see it. Usually, though, I tape a stiff cardboard top on mine to keep scenery materials from falling on the track later when I build the hill above the tunnel.

Pour plaster (Woodland Scenics lightweight Hydrocal takes detail extremely well) in a rubber rock mold large enough to overlap the tunnel opening by several inches. (Woodland Scenics also has some big rock molds.)

When the plaster begins to set, place the mold against the false face and hold it in position for 10 or 15 minutes, or until the plaster has begun to set, and you can safely pull off the rubber mold. Don't press too hard, and don't press at all against the portion of the casting that covers the tunnel opening.

Once the plaster has set, but before it hardens, begin gingerly chipping away the tunnel mouth with a small screwdriver, hobby knife, or whatever else works. Go for that neat effect where you see some of the liner edge showing, as in the photo.

Tom Danneman

To model the stratified rock surrounding this tunnel portal, look for an appropriate rubber mold that will yield the horizontal striations. You can reinforce the look with some subtle carving while the plaster is still soft enough to work.

47

The tunnel entrance on the other side of the bluff, seen here in 1952, sports a handsome stone portal with heavy buttresses projecting from each side of the opening to help hold back the hillside. As tunnel portals go, this one is small with interesting detail, so it makes an excellent modeling candidate. One approach would be to start with a Woodland Scenics no. 1253 cut stone portal. Using a razor saw you could cut and fit pieces from Woodland Scenics no. 1259 cut stone retaining walls to represent the buttresses and abbreviated wing walls. (The N scale equivalents are nos. 1153 and 1159.)

Henry J. McCord

This proud little tunnel portal wouldn't require much room on your layout.

Oh, my! Misfortune had befallen the southside portal sometime before this steam excursion passed through in 1961. The top of the arch has either collapsed or been removed by the railroad. If a modeling project doesn't work out to suit you, you can always resort to something like this. A demolition or construction scene always adds lots of interest to a layout. It amounts to history in the making.

Our best guess is the railroad heightened the portal, and maybe the entire tunnel, to provide more vertical clearance for trains passing through.

J. David Ingles

48

Chuck Porter

KEY MATERIALS

Concrete tunnel liner
Thick styrene sheet (.080") or ¼" foam board

Rockwork
Woodland Scenics lightweight Hydrocal
Woodland Scenics rubber rock molds (also available from others)

Tunnel portals
Woodland Scenics no. 1253 cut stone portal (HO); no. 1153 (N)
Woodland Scenics no. 1259 cut stone retaining walls (HO); no. 1159 (N)

This photo taken in 1986 appears to bear out our theory that the tunnel was heightened.

This October 30, 1986 shot completes our little tale of the East Dubuque portal. The original stone arch has been replaced with one made of poured concrete. We wonder if those cars on the left belong to railfans who climbed the bluff and never returned.

EAST DUBUQUE CONCEPT
HO, 24"-minimum-radius curves

Swing-down bridge for access

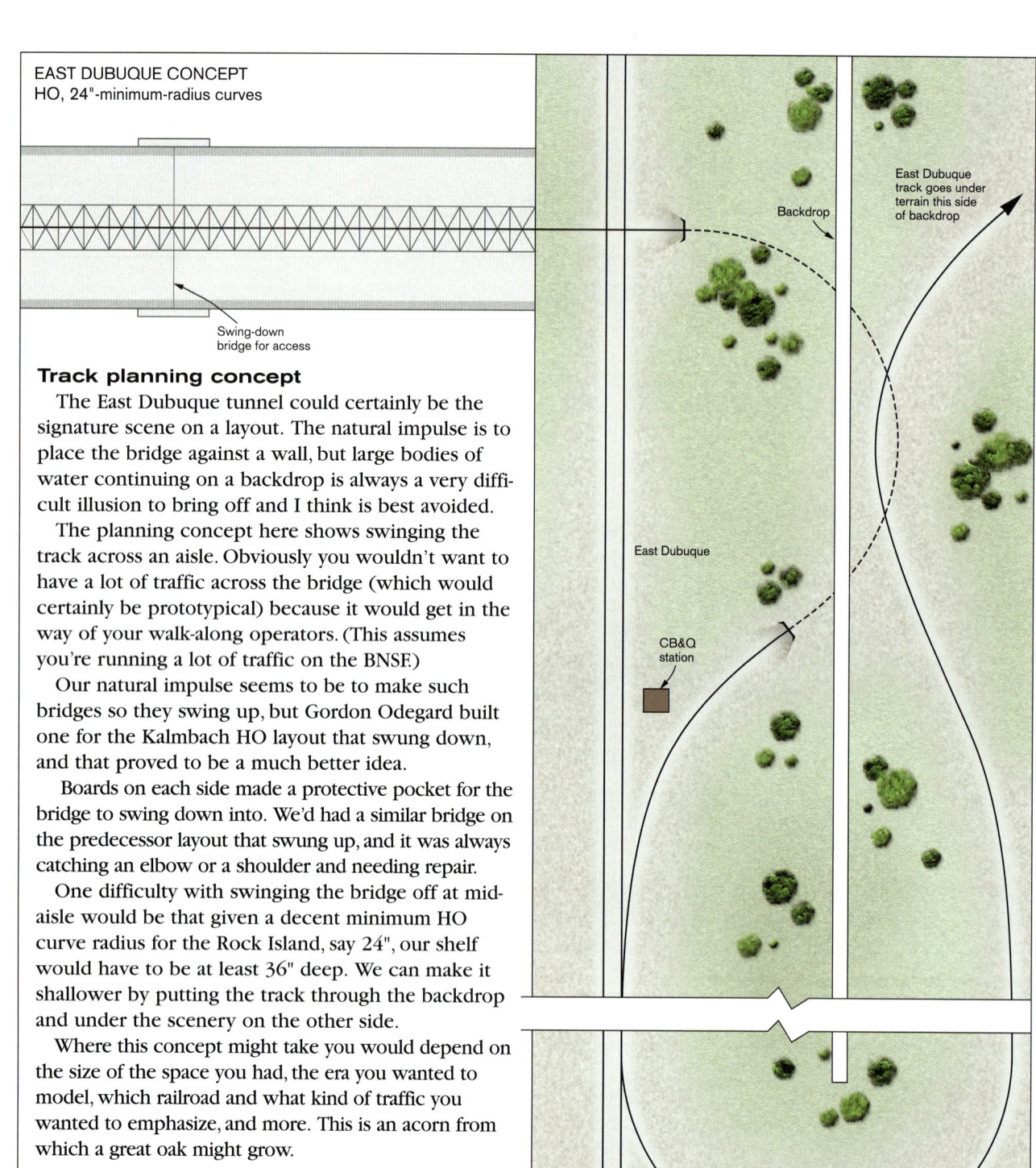

Backdrop

East Dubuque track goes under terrain this side of backdrop

East Dubuque

CB&Q station

Track planning concept

The East Dubuque tunnel could certainly be the signature scene on a layout. The natural impulse is to place the bridge against a wall, but large bodies of water continuing on a backdrop is always a very difficult illusion to bring off and I think is best avoided.

The planning concept here shows swinging the track across an aisle. Obviously you wouldn't want to have a lot of traffic across the bridge (which would certainly be prototypical) because it would get in the way of your walk-along operators. (This assumes you're running a lot of traffic on the BNSF.)

Our natural impulse seems to be to make such bridges so they swing up, but Gordon Odegard built one for the Kalmbach HO layout that swung down, and that proved to be a much better idea.

Boards on each side made a protective pocket for the bridge to swing down into. We'd had a similar bridge on the predecessor layout that swung up, and it was always catching an elbow or a shoulder and needing repair.

One difficulty with swinging the bridge off at mid-aisle would be that given a decent minimum HO curve radius for the Rock Island, say 24", our shelf would have to be at least 36" deep. We can make it shallower by putting the track through the backdrop and under the scenery on the other side.

Where this concept might take you would depend on the size of the space you had, the era you wanted to model, which railroad and what kind of traffic you wanted to emphasize, and more. This is an acorn from which a great oak might grow.

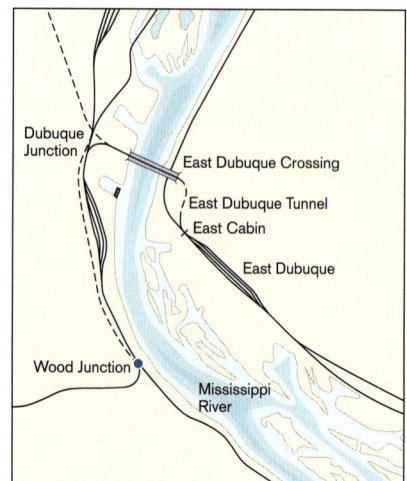

Dubuque Junction
East Dubuque Crossing
East Dubuque Tunnel
East Cabin
East Dubuque
Wood Junction
Mississippi River

50

Mr. Lincoln for the defense

By the late 1850s, several railroads were poised to bridge the Mississippi River, but first they wanted to see how the Rock Island Railroad fared in its courtroom battles against anti-bridge interests. In 1856 at Rock Island, Ill., the Rock had completed the first railroad bridge across the Mississippi. Most citizens in Iowa and points west, especially farmers and others with products to sell back east, were jubilant, but the steamboat operators didn't like it one little bit.

Within two weeks the Effie Afton, a steamboat out of St. Louis, made a suspiciously sloppy run through the bridge's draw span, ramming a pier, catching fire, and wrecking one span of the bridge. Steamboat interests seized upon this "accident" to take the Rock Island to court in an effort to have the bridge removed. The boat people argued that the bridge was a crime against nature, that they had been there first and had "priority" rights, and that bridges anywhere on the river posed hazards to navigation. They feared that someday there would be bridges every 40 miles or so all up and down the river. (And, of course, they turned out to be right.)

The railroad's legal team was led by Abraham Lincoln, who went to Rock Island and conducted experiments which he claimed demonstrated that the wreck, given the river currents, had to be intentional. Lincoln relied heavily on an engineering study that had been prepared by a U.S. Army officer from Virginia, Robert E. Lee.

Lincoln didn't win, but he didn't lose either— the jury couldn't decide. Next the steamboat interests went to the U.S. district court in Iowa and won. The court ruled the Iowa half of the bridge had to be torn down.

Rather than get out the wrecking ball, the Rock Island went to the United States Supreme Court and won a decision that established for all time the right to bridge navigable streams. By this time it was 1860, Mr. Lincoln's attention had shifted to trying to hold the Union together, and the railroads' plans for further expansion were postponed until after the Civil War was over.

BRIDGES

Chuck Porter

Serving Huckleberry's hometown

Three generations of bridges

The Mississippi River bridge at Hannibal, Mo., was completed in 1871 and first used by the Toledo, Wabash & Western, which in 1877 became part of the Wabash. Nowadays the bridge serves the Norfolk Southern, and little of the original structure remains. The original swing bridge was replaced in the 1990s by a lift bridge.

The Hannibal bridge makes an interesting contrast with the Dubuque, Iowa, bridge we looked at earlier. They were built at about the same time, but the Hannibal bridge has served larger railroad companies with a lot more traffic and has been modernized over the years, while the Dubuque bridge has remained frozen in time.

In the Chuck Porter photo above, it's July 12, 1989, and after a long and quite complicated history, the former Wabash (which became part of the Norfolk & Western in 1964) has been part of the Norfolk

The Hannibal bridge has been updated several times.

Southern since 1982. The Hannibal bridge, painted black in earlier years, is now a spiffy silver. To the right is the swing bridge that accommodated river traffic. The trusses towards the Illinois side are considerably heavier than those you'll see in pictures taken earlier.

In the late 1950s, legendary *Model Railroader* Magazine editor Linn Westcott shot this fascinating down-on photo of the Wabash's Mississippi River crossing at Hannibal, Mo. Those curved "curbs" at the end of the bridge are almost certainly the tops of retaining walls.

Note the close tie spacing on the bridge track. Both Walthers and Micro Engineering offer such track in HO flextrack; the guard rails are incorporated into it. The 36" Micro Engineering sections are the more economical, while the Walthers bridge tracks are expressly designed to fit their bridges. Micro Engineering also offers N scale bridge track in both codes 70 and 55, also in 36" lengths with the guard rails incorporated.

Note the plank walkway down one side of the rails. It made the bridge tender's walk to work much easier and safer and could be modeled with stripwood.

And how about those track workers on the speeder commuting to work? The railroad crossing the Wabash here on the Missouri side of the river is the Chicago, Burlington & Quincy.

Linn Westcott

Here's a fascinating 1950s down-on photo of the Wabash's Mississippi River crossing atHannibal, Mo.

The single-tracked Hannibal bridge presents a unique modeling challenge.

At first glance here's a situation for that Walthers Cornerstone no. 3088 HO swing bridge you'd like to have on the layout. Unfortunately, the Walthers bridge is double-tracked and our prototype is single. Model railroaders, an ingenious lot, could, I'm sure, figure out how to narrow the bridge.

The long structures up- and downstream are designed to protect the bridge ends from off-target boats. (Remember the bridge is pointing up- and downriver when the bridge is open.) Made of pilings and timbers, they need to be longer than the bridge's span. Note the safety striping on the end panels and the debris piled up by the current.

53

This 1946 photo shows the extensive control house built at the center of the swing span in earlier years and the enclosed stairway that led up it. The bridge tender was also responsible for all the signals in the bridge area.

Styrene shacks would work for a swing bridge's control cabin.

Henry J. McCord

It's 1948 as a Wabash class B-7 steam locomotive exits Hannibal's 100-foot-long tunnel through the bluff. Driving your car across here required an act of faith, although the crossing gate's failsafe position is down, and any approaching train will be going no faster than 5 mph. A Woodland Scenics cut stone tunnel portal (no 1253 HO, 1153 N) would have you well on your way to modeling this scene.

A stone portal can be simple and doesn't have to have wings.

J.M. Gray

Linn stepped inside the tunnel to get this interesting shot. It provides us a good reference for a highway crossing at grade. This one is just timbers to each side of the rails plus one in the middle, with gravel or asphalt to fill the area between the timbers. Note also the simple construction of the handcar set-out right and just short of the road. A little stained stripwood is all you'd need to represent it.

Note that more-modern crossing gates have replaced those shown in the photo above.

Linn H. Westcott

KEY MATERIALS

Bridge tracks
Walthers and Micro Engineering flextrack (HO)
Micro Engineering track in both codes 70 and 55 (N)

Plank walkway
Stripwood

Swing bridge
Walthers Cornerstone no. 3088 (HO)

Tunnel portal
Woodland Scenics no. 1253 (HO) or no. 1153 (N) cut stone tunnel portal

Handcar set-out
Stripwood

If you visit the bridge site today, you'll find the swing bridge has been replaced by a modern lift bridge and the road across the face of the tunnel has been closed.

Today's lift bridges are less susceptible to damage from barge traffic than swing bridges were.

J. David Ingles

Here's the other end of today's lift bridge. The stone piers have now been replaced with concrete. The lift bridge is shorter than the old 120-foot swing bridge; a short through-girder bridge makes up the difference.

With no central pivot pier, a lift bridge can be shorter than a swing type and still provide more room for passage.

J. David Ingles

This modern structure now governs the diamond and the lift bridge. The protective screen is there to thwart vandals who might throw rocks from the city park across the track and atop the bluff.

Today's bridge tender works in this spartan structure.

J. David Ingles

55

TUNNELS AND SHELF SCENES

Jim Kelly

Now you see it, now you don't

SP's tunnels at Tehachapi

Ask model railroaders, especially those just starting out, what they'd like on their layouts, and bridges and tunnels are almost sure to be included. Both are inherently interesting because they accent the relationship between the railroad's right-of-way and the terrain. The railroad has to stay on a fairly constant plane, but the land is free to rise and fall abruptly.

Sometimes the railroad dominates the scene with long high fills, deep cuts, and long tunnels that save miles of winding and climbing. Other times the line is more at one with nature, blending in and rolling and turning with the hilly terrain.

My favorite chunk of railroad real estate, the Union Pacific's 68-mile route over the Tehachapi Mountains, includes 12 tunnels. (In my heart it's still a Southern Pacific property as the SP built it and ran it until the railroad was bought by the UP in 1998.) Once there were 18 tunnels on the line, including a Tunnel ½ that was built to accommodate a line shift some 25 years after the railroad was completed in 1876.

Six of these tunnels, including Tunnel ½, have since been daylighted (i.e., the top opened up, making a cut instead of a tunnel). The Southern Pacific opened four of

Here's the long view of Tunnel 14's east portal near Tehachapi.

them to the skies of its own volition, but Nature lent a hand on numbers 4 and 6 (and part of number 3) with a massive earthquake on July 21, 1952.

The Tehachapi tunnels aren't long as tunnels go, but they're all photogenic, the track inside nearly all of them curves, and they all show the effects of time. Despite the similarities of their simple cast concrete portals, they are all different and interesting. Some are easy to get to (nos. 2, 3, 9, and 10), while others are seldom seen except by

Tunnel 16, like all the Tehachapi Pass photos show, features a plain poured concrete portal.

SP trackworkers and UP and Burlington Northern Santa Fe engine crews. (The Santa Fe gained running rights on the line in 1899 and has retained them ever since.)

Four of these tunnels, nos. 14, 15, 16, and 17, are near the top of the long, hard haul from Bakersfield to the town of Tehachapi, and you'll see them flanking the mountain on your left if you drive on busy Highway 5 from Tehachapi to Bakersfield. You'll also see the famous Tehachapi Loop another five miles or so down the road, if you know where to look.

The railroad follows Tehachapi Creek as best it can, but has to take a more roundabout route because the creek drops so rapidly. The railroad's builders hacked out a shelf on the mountainsides and tunneled through the ridges that stand out from the side of the mountain like flying buttresses. (Many of the workers were Chinese or veterans of Charlie Crocker's legendary crews that built the first transcontinental railroad's route over Donner Pass.)

Modeling thoughts

A series of short tunnels like these (far shorter than these, actually) could add spice to lots of model railroading situations. Take, for example, a long mountain grade either entirely in the open or entirely inside a tunnel and built on a shelf. The first could be dull, yet as much as model railroaders like tunnels, they generally don't like really long ones very well and get antsy wondering if the train is still running and sometimes even if it's going to reappear where they have assumed it will.

What the photos show

The long view of Tunnel 14's east portal (opposite) captures the essence of the four short tunnels near the top of the Union Pacific's line from Bakersfield to Mojave. On the right is Tehachapi Creek, which carved a route down the mountain that a railroad could generally follow. This is high desert country and most of the time the creek is dry, or nearly so, with what water there is often flowing beneath the gravelly surface. As the boulders in the stream attest, though, when heavy rains come to the Tehachapis, the creek can become a highly destructive torrent. (It once swept away a steam locomotive and buried it completely in mud.)

On the far side of the creek is the freeway—California highway 58. Note the stone retaining wall that helps prevent the road from sliding into the creek. A curved retaining wall like this is probably most easily achieved by first making a plain wall from thin but flexible sheet styrene (.040" should be about right) and then cementing on a face of plastic stone sheet. Kibri, Noch, Faller, and others all make such material. You'll need to cement the wall against wood formers to hold the curve, then scenick it in.

Tunnel 16 (photo above) has suffered the indignity of having the bottom of its right wing knocked out of the way to make room for an access road. Like most mountain railroads over the past 50 years, the Southern Pacific has done a considerable amount of bulldozing to make its line accessible to off-road vehicles. This is particularly important on the SP's Tehachapi route as the line is single-tracked and very busy. You don't want track space and time taken up by maintenance vehicles.

Many of the more-recent photos in this book, taken all over the country, reveal how important access roads have become to the railroad scene. They are generally

57

no wider and no better maintained than absolutely necessary, and they make interesting model subjects. In fact, a model of a modern railroad doesn't look quite right without them.

This closeup shot of tunnel 16's east portal shows lots of interesting detail. Note the form lines in the concrete and the vertical streaking caused by the rains washing the grime down the surfaces. The Tehachapis see lots of traffic and lots of hard-working locomotives (often a dozen or more on a train) so the portal area above the rathole is always black with smoke.

Tehachapi tunnels are so rudimentary that no commercial portals resemble them. They're just a plain concrete wall with a simple cap. The easiest approach is to make a simple rubber mold, cast your own, and then modify each one to fit its location. What adds variety and makes the tunnels so interesting is all the wing wall configurations, built to suit the particular situation and often modified over time.

Tunnel 16's east portal exhibits telling discolorations.

The east portal for Tunnel 15 sits right next to a solid rock outcropping and so required no wing wall to the left. The wing on the right features an interesting stair-step shape. Part of the crowning ledge above the rathole has fallen away. In the mid-1990s the SP spent millions of dollars increasing the clearances in the Tehachapi tunnels so they could accommodate double-stack intermodal cars. They dug the tunnel floors deeper (the easiest way to increase clearance in tunnels) and also carved some concrete off the ceilings. On some portals, small notches were cut into the portal's arch so those double-stacked containers could slip through.

Tunnel 15's east portal was built right next to a solid rock outcropping.

Jim Kelly

Tunnel 17 has wings projecting forward from each side of the portal. The fence posts and power poles marching up and over the hill would be interesting details to add to any tunnel scene. We wonder why nothing will grow on that bare slope just under the locomotives. At any rate it's a sight to keep in mind for adding variety to your scenery. Notice how different the plant life is here from what you'll see later when we get to the Loop.

Tunnel 17 on the Southern Pacific's Tehachapi route exhibit several interesting detail elements.

KEY MATERIALS

Curved retaining wall
Sheet styrene: 040"
Kibri, Noch, or Faller plastic stone sheet

59

TUNNELS AND SHELF SCENES

Up against the wall

The perfect mountain scene

Having convinced you, I hope, that short tunnels are a good way to add interest to a long shelf scene running in open country, let's look at some more possibili-ties. Here are two idyllic scenes that are as big as all outdoors, but both could easily be modeled on a narrow shelf, say 18" deep in HO or 12" in N.

Tunnels and cuts add interest by raising the land above the trains. Fills and bridges play their part by dropping it below. Here's an east-bound Burlington Northern train

60

Kurt Heiden

This stunning scene captured at East Glacier, Mont., would be perfect on a model railroad.

crossing Two Medicine Creek at East Glacier, Mont., on the former Great Northern Railroad. The more I look at railfan photos taken in Montana, the more I become convinced that the entire state is one magnificent model railroad backdrop. Certainly that's the case here. Everything above the train looks exactly like a painted backdrop.

You could build the long bridge within a few inches of the backdrop and represent the rest with painting. And you wouldn't have to be a great artist to represent what you see here, thanks mostly to the line of dark green pine trees that makes a handy transition to the mountains in the background.

In his book *How to Build Model Railroad Scenery* (Kalmbach Publishing Co.), Dave Frary shows step-by-step how to paint backdrops. The major principle is that he works forward in vertical planes. For a backdrop like this, he would paint the sky first, then the distant mountains, then the evergreens, working forward so that each "layer" goes partially over the one that came before.

The steel trestle shouts Micro Engineering kits, both in HO and N; we discussed using those several chapters back.

Just to contradict myself a bit, even though you could model this scene on a narrow shelf, the more foreground you could give it the better. The beauty of it is you can drop the foreground rapidly towards the front of the layout, giving you a lot of scenick effect in a shallow space. A really neat feature is the way the trees lead your eye under the bridge, and also off to the left, very handy for hiding the base of our backdrop.

Note how "model railroady" the landscape already looks. To achieve that look, just paint the surface with a flat tan latex paint and sprinkle on some medium green ground foam, letting quite a bit of tan show through.

And what's with those circular grassy areas on the slope to the right? Have we stumbled across a landing site left by alien interlopers? Whatever they are, those round patches would be neat to model. Just paint on a circle of thinned white glue, matte medium, or Woodland Scenics scenery cement and sprinkle on a little Woodland Scenics turf.

The old barn gives you an opportunity to get a little funky. Good N scale possibilities include Showcase Miniatures no. 115 Deloney's farm, Northeastern no. 30009 dairy barn (which is rather like the barn in the photo), American Models no. 619, and Model Power no. 1517. For HO you could choose among Dyna-Model no. 309, IHC no. 812, Northeastern 40009, and Pola 569.

Dan Poitras

The Burlington Northern passes through a series of cuts made in long, low ridges in Crawford, Nebr.

This shot was taken east of Crawford, Nebr., in May of 1998. The rocky ridges buttressing the hill to the left weren't high enough to require tunneling, so they were breached with cuts. Also, the rock here was hard and consistent enough that it could be cut through with relative ease, and the cut faces would remain stable. (One of the challenges in the Tehachapis was that the terrain was sometimes a jumble of rocks and dirt that wouldn't remain stable once disturbed.)

Imagine a giant hand laid on the hill to the left and you can see that the railroad has cut through the fingers. Picture the scene from the right looking at the track perpendicularly and you can see the interesting possibilities for shelf scenery. One intriguing approach would be to model a series of progressively deeper cuts like these until reaching taller ridges which you then tunnel through.

Former *Model Railroader* Magazine editor Linn Westcott would often speculate about building the layout's scenery first, then excavating and filling for the roadbed. Certainly that would be prototypical (real railroads had no choice), but I always felt that approach would take a lot of extra work, and the scenery builder with an average eye and skills would get the same result. Still, this might be an interesting situation for trying Linn's approach, although I'd cheat and have my subroadbed in position first.

This photograph, taken back east at Alfred Station, N.Y., includes many of the same modelgenic qualities seen in the BN in Montana shot. Again the bridge could be quite near the backdrop. Painting this backdrop would be more of a challenge, though, especially if you wanted to model the autumn scenery shown here. For the bare trees, you might draw a few on paper, then have rubber stamps made. Some art and architectural stores already have such stamps. Then use various shades of gray, brown, and black to "stamp" yourself a forest. Just go easy with the ink. You'd want to use something of a "dry-stamping" technique.

Note the stone wall supporting the track to the right. Chooch has walls in both HO and N scales that would represent it nicely. Besides being a handsome and interesting feature, this could be handy on a layout for hiding something, let's say the creek, by bending it sharply to the right, thus avoiding that difficult transition into the backdrop. Also interesting are the steel bars to the far right, helping keep the railroad from sliding into the creek.

The bridge is our old friend, the deck girder. I'd guess there's a bridge or abutment behind that golden tree because this bridge is about as long as it can be given the depth of the girder. In HO I'd use Central Valley's no. 1903 bridge to represent it. In N you could use Micro Engineering's no. 75150 open deck or no. 75152 ballasted 80-foot deck girder bridges. You also have the option of buying just the girders (80170) and gluing them to the sides of your roadbed.

Charles Woolever

This Alfred Station, N.Y., photo includes many of the same modelgenic qualities seen in the photo on pages 58 and 59.

This splendid set of bridges, photographed in 1990, is located on the CSX at Joppatown, Md. Note the buttresses on the sides of the arches. You could make a similar bridge in HO using Faller's no. 545 arch bridge and no. 547 piers. A second set of piers could be kitbashed to make the buttresses for the pier sides. Faller's no. 2585 should work in N scale, as should Atlas's no. 2826.

Atlas's deck truss bridge (no. 884 in HO, no. 2547) could be used as is or kitbashed a little to more closely resemble the prototype.

Note again how bridge styles can be mixed.

Stephen Panopoulos

63

John Uckley

Placing a pier in the middle of the stream allowed for shallow girders here on Otter Creek.

Now here's a handsome and very basic deck girder bridge photographed in December of 1981 on Otter Creek near LaSalle, Michigan. A neat trick to try here, assuming the bridge was quite near the wall, would be to cut the piers and abutments in half and place a mirror flush against the joints so that the stream in the foreground is reflected and appears to keep on going. You just wouldn't want the bridge at eye level, otherwise what you would see would be your own eyes peering back at you.

KEY MATERIALS

Steel trestle
Micro Engineering kits in HO and N
High desert scenery
Flat tan latex paint
Medium green ground foam
Circular grassy areas
Thinned white glue
Matte medium or Woodland Scenics scenery cement
Woodland Scenics turf
Barn
Dyna-Model no. 309, IHC no. 812, Northeastern 40009, and Pola 569 (HO)
Showcase Miniatures no. 115 Deloney's farm, Northeastern no. 30009 dairy barn, American Models no. 619, and Model Power no. 1517 (N)
Bare trees
Rubber stamps custom made
Stone wall
Chooch in both HO and N
Deck girder
Central Valley no. 1903 bridge (HO)
Micro Engineering no. 75150 open deck or no. 75152 ballasted 80-footer (N)
Bridge with buttresses
Faller's no. 545 arch bridge and no. 547 piers (HO)
Faller's no. 2585 (N)
Atlas no. 2826 (N)
Culvert
Campbell aluminum siding strips rolled around a dowel
Walthers Goo
½" dowel—pipe 44" in diameter for HO

Alex Mayes

A highway underpass is always good for breaking up the sameness of a long run on a shelf and can also provide a good place to show off better trucks or cars. You could even set up a mini-scene, perhaps involving an overheated radiator or a blown tire. This scene was shot May 23, 1987, on the Denver & Rio Grande Western's main line about a mile east of the Moffet tunnel.

An easy solution for a ballasted deck bridge like this is just to glue a girder to the side of the roadbed. You might even (shudder) scratch-build the girder, as the one on the far side can't be seen and needs no detail. All you would have to do is cement Evergreen's styrene angle to sheet styrene. The railings could be made using angle for the stanchions and strip for the rails. Don't skip the culvert to the left of the photo. It'll add a lot of interest and keep your fill from washing out.

I don't know of any galvanized steel pipe available on the market, but you can make your own by rolling strips of Campbell aluminum siding around a dowel. Wrap a paper test strip around the dowel to determine how long the material needs to be in order for the ends to overlap by $\frac{1}{16}$", then cut the aluminum siding accordingly.

I'd apply a little Walthers Goo on opposite sides at each end of the strip, let it set a minute, then wrap the strip around the dowel and press the ends to glue them together. A $\frac{1}{2}$" dowel would give you a pipe 44" in diameter for HO, about right for the scene here.

You could use a mirror under a bridge like this to create the illusion of a continuing road.

65

ALONG THE LINE

Jim Kelly

Round in circles we go

The Tehachapi Loop

Anyone who knows me knows I could never write a book like this without including the Tehachapi Loop. It's my favorite trainwatching spot, hands down, and has been the centerpiece of the three N scale layouts I've built since 1980. Lest I forget that not everyone knows of this railfanning mecca, let alone will have made the pilgrimage, let me elaborate.

The Loop is located on the Union Pacific's main line between Tehachapi and Bakersfield, Calif., right off route 58. (Exit for Keene and the signs will direct you to the Loop, which is about two miles away.)

The photo above shows what the Loop looks like. You can quickly see why the Loop hill has sometimes been compared to the work of an inept model railroader. It's just too regular and "pointy" to look real. Note the long fill extending from behind the hill to above Tunnel 9. (See the map on page 70.) This long Southern Pacific train easily crossed its tail on the Loop. The photo was taken in May of 1983, and the scenery is still green from the spring rains. Come back in August and you'll find the area parched and brown.

William Hood, who laid out the Southern Pacific's tortuous route over the Tehachapi Mountains in the 1870s saw the Loop as no great achievement. The railroad just went around in a circle and crossed over itself. To him it was simply a common sense solution

This long view of the Tehachapi Loop shows the "model railroad-like" Loop hill.

to the problem of needing to gain elevation (75 feet as it turned out) without going much of anywhere, but it's been regarded ever since as a stroke of engineering genius.

The more I look at photos of the Loop, the more I find interesting features that aren't immediately obvious. For example, while it's true that the Loop goes up and around a conveniently situated (and rather phony looking) hill, a lot of earth had to be rearranged to make it possible. Considerable blasting was done on the back of the hill, resulting in an interesting terraced face that we don't often see in photos.

Also, a lot of earth had to be moved to dig the trench at the base of the hill, which allows the trains to cross over themselves. And once the line has circled the hill, it runs on a high fill all the way over to where it crosses Tunnel 9.

To sum it up, what Hood saw when he looked at this location and what we see today are quite different. We see the result; he saw the possibility. It truly was an inspired moment.

Here's the view from on top of Tunnel 9 and looking up the hill. Walong siding begins here, as indicated by the sign, and runs nearly all the way to Tunnel 10, which can be made out on the distant hill. The searchlight signal is for uphill trains. Note the electrically powered switch machine next to it. The Tehachapi route is governed by CTC (Centralized Traffic Control), and the signals and switches are set by a dispatcher far away. The signal bridge just around the bend is for downhill trains. The wood stairway leads to the track above and can save crew members a lot of walking when there's a problem somewhere in the train.

Details like those seen from atop Tunnel 9 will add realism to a layout.

The north side of the Loop hill had to be cut back considerably and contrasts extremely with the smooth southern slope. This shot was taken in 1986. Since 1989 a white cross has stood at the top of the hill to memorialize the lives of Southern Pacific and Santa Fe railroaders who lost their lives on the job. Note the service road cut into the rock face. The hill was cut back in a series of three terraces.

A great deal of excavation was required to create the Tehachapi Loop, as is shown in this shot of the north side of the loop hill.

Tunnel 9 is the short tunnel (126 feet long) that leads uphill trains into the Loop. To support the track above Tunnel 9 a considerable fill was required. Tunnel portals don't get any more basic than those used on Tehachapi Pass. Note how the access road goes up to the right of the portal, then crosses behind it. As we noted earlier, such roads often are not particularly attractive, but they are a vital part of the modern railroad scene. Gravel or dirt, they're not hard to blend into

Typical freight trains usually cross their own tails at Tunnel 9.

the terrain and afford a place to show off some interesting vehicles, including those driven by foolhardy railfans.

Railfans get to the Loop any which way they can, and often you'll meet folks from all over the world there. The portal at Tunnel 10, just above the Loop, is braced with wing walls that help keep rock off the track. It's also small as tunnel portals go (only about 25 feet tall) and would make a good prototype for a place where you need a model and just don't have much room.

These morotcycles, most likely belonging to railfans, would add interest to a small tunnel scene, like the Tunnel 10 portal, just above the Loop.

68

Got a ranch somewhere on your layout? A sign like the one for the Loop Ranch might be just the ticket for establishing some western identity, maybe with a few head of cattle grazing inside the fence. Three-dimensional letters can be hard to find, but two manufacturers are Slater Plastikard and Scalelink. Both are British companies, but bigger U.S. hobby shops do sometimes have their products. The ranch buildings could be "off the layout," and you wouldn't necessarily have to model them. Consider this a good place to show off a pickup truck and a horse trailer.

Modeling this sign for the Loop Ranch would establish a layout's western identity.

This homebuilt ramp serves for unloading flatcars off the end of the short spur on the Loop. All you need to make a ramp like this is some spare railroad ties, such as those provided by Campbell, Kappler, or Micro Engineering. Old maps show that this track was once double-ended for a second passing track on the Loop.

This homebuilt ramp, mostly used to unload tracklaying supplies, would be an easy one-evening modeling project.

69

MODELING WALONG IN N SCALE
18"-minimum-radius curves

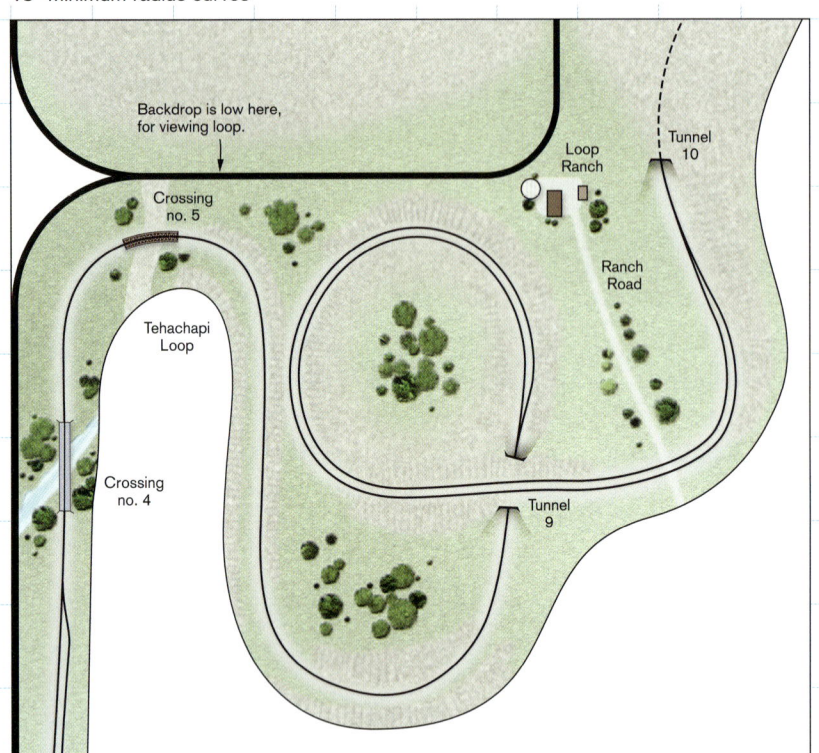

KEY MATERIALS

Sign for the Loop Ranch
Slater Plastikard and Scalelink three-dimensional letters

Homebuilt ramp
Campbell, Kappler, or Micro Engineering railroad ties

A Tehachapi track-planning concept

You can always use a loop on a layout to achieve the same objective William Hood did—to gain elevation. It's a one-turn helix and could be particularly effective at the end of a peninsula where you have to have a turnback curve anyway.

On my first two layouts, both double-deckers, I was using the Loop and the approaches to it to make the 18" climb between decks. When John Armstrong visited, he took one look and said, "It's just a helix out in the open."

Unless at the end of a peninsula, a loop introduces space problems. In HO scale, assuming a decent radius, let's say 36", the loop would be so far across that you'd either need to situate it so you can reach it from all sides or install a pop-up hatch. Even in N, assuming an 18" radius, you'd have a hard time reaching to the middle. Of course, there's no track or anything else essential in there, so it's not a major concern.

Ultimately, I'd like to have a loop that can be viewed from all the way around. The section of track plan shown above is getting there, and if the top of the backdrop is low enough that you can look over it, then you are there. What you would do with the rest of the layout would depend on the space you have and your operating goals. My own Loop is stashed in the attic awaiting its move to a new basement.

ALONG THE LINE

George Drury

Ace of diamonds

Rochelle Railroad Park

Rochelle, Ill., is a farm town some 90 miles west of Chicago near the intersection of I-88 and I-39. It's a pleasant enough town in flat, rich Illinois corn country, but you probably wouldn't have much occasion to go there if you weren't a railfan. You are, though, and so for you it's a destination not to be missed.

That's because heavily traveled, double-tracked main lines of the nation's last two great western railroads, the Burlington Northern Santa Fe and the Union Pacific, cross there. (Before 1998 they were Burlington Northern and Chicago & North Western routes.)

Ken Wise recognized what a treasure this crossing could be for the town of Rochelle, and he led the way in establishing the Rochelle Railroad Park. A raised pavilion to the east of the diamonds provides some relief from the weather and an ideal location for photography or for just kicking back and enjoying the trains. There's also a small hobby shop on the site, to which you can risk a quick visit, although you may miss a train in the process.

A feature like Rochelle on a model railroad could be just the ticket for the modeler who isn't content with just one major railroad and wants two! Both could be prototype, or one or both could be free-lance. The Boston & Maine crossing the Santa Fe wouldn't be very convincing, but if your two lines run in the same part of the country, why not?

There's a lot of standardization in today's railroading. All major railroads run the same locomotive

The diamonds at Rochelle: high on the list of places you'd least like to have a derailment.

types, for example, but still there are lots of interesting differences. For instance, you can still see UP's C&NW heritage in the Pink Lady ballast. The pinkish rock came from a quarry in west-central Wisconsin and was used all over the system. The BNSF's ballast is a more typical gray. Both lines protect the crossing in both directions with signal bridges, but those on the BNSF carry round targets while those on the UP are oval-shaped.

On a layout, you'd probably want to feature the railroad you're most interested in and make the other one a secondary line. The track-planning concept on page 74 offers some possibilities.

Here's a shot taken at Rochelle in October of 1986, a decade before the present-day railroad park was built. Pink was a popular color choice for owners of large grain elevators all across the Midwest who had to meet the car shortage by providing their own. Those cars certainly stood out, particularly as the elevator company's name usually appeared in large block letters running nearly the length of the car. Steve was able to take such a good photo because he stood nearer the diamond and was able to eliminate the power poles, relay boxes, and other clutter, which are actually of considerable interest to the modeler.

Steve Karlson

That canning company beyond the diamonds was built to fit the oddly-shaped site.

It was December of 2002 when these eastbound UP locomotives cleared the diamonds and were photographed passing under the signal bridge governing westbound traffic. Notice how the higher targets are basically ground-type signals mounted on platforms built on the bridge. This is a former Chicago & North Western route, and true to its heritage, the trains still favor the left-hand track on a double-track main, contrary to the practice of virtually every other American railroad. This is a useful piece of information only if you're modeling C&NW-related prototypes, but a good example of the kind of information you can make use of to make your model railroad authentic.

Jim Kelly

With Chicago straight ahead, this Eastbound UP locomotive clears the diamonds at Rochelle.

Here's a westbound BNSF approaching the diamonds. Note that the signal targets on this former Burlington Northern (earlier Chicago, Burlington & Quincy) line are round. The gray ballast seen here is an interesting contrast to the "Pink Lady" stone on the UP.

The trees to the right here could be painted on a backdrop.

Jim Kelly

72

Rochelle was the home of Whitcomb Locomotive Works, so the railroad park includes a surviving Whitcomb locomotive displayed under a simple, open structure. The idea would be easy to overdo, but you could probably find a logical spot or two on your own layout to display some older or unusual equipment.

A Whitcomb industrial locomotive pays tribute to Rochelle's history.

Jim Kelly

Another bit of history displayed at Rochelle is this short specimen of re-created strap track dating back to the very early days of railroading. Steel strap was spiked to lengths of timber. This type of track was outlawed early on because the strap would wreak havoc if it worked loose and got up into the floors of cars. These dreaded "snakeheads" were especially hazardous to passengers riding in early wood-floored coaches.

Rail history displays could give your railfans something to look at between trains.

Jim Kelly

In this photo, we're looking east towards the Rochelle pavilion. On a sunny weekend day in the summer, you'll usually find dozens of railfans enjoying the action in comfort and safety. Note the massive stones used to build up the pavilion's platform. They were probably reclaimed from some structure on the railroad.

Tthe Rochelle pavilion is a great train-watching spot.

Jim Kelly

73

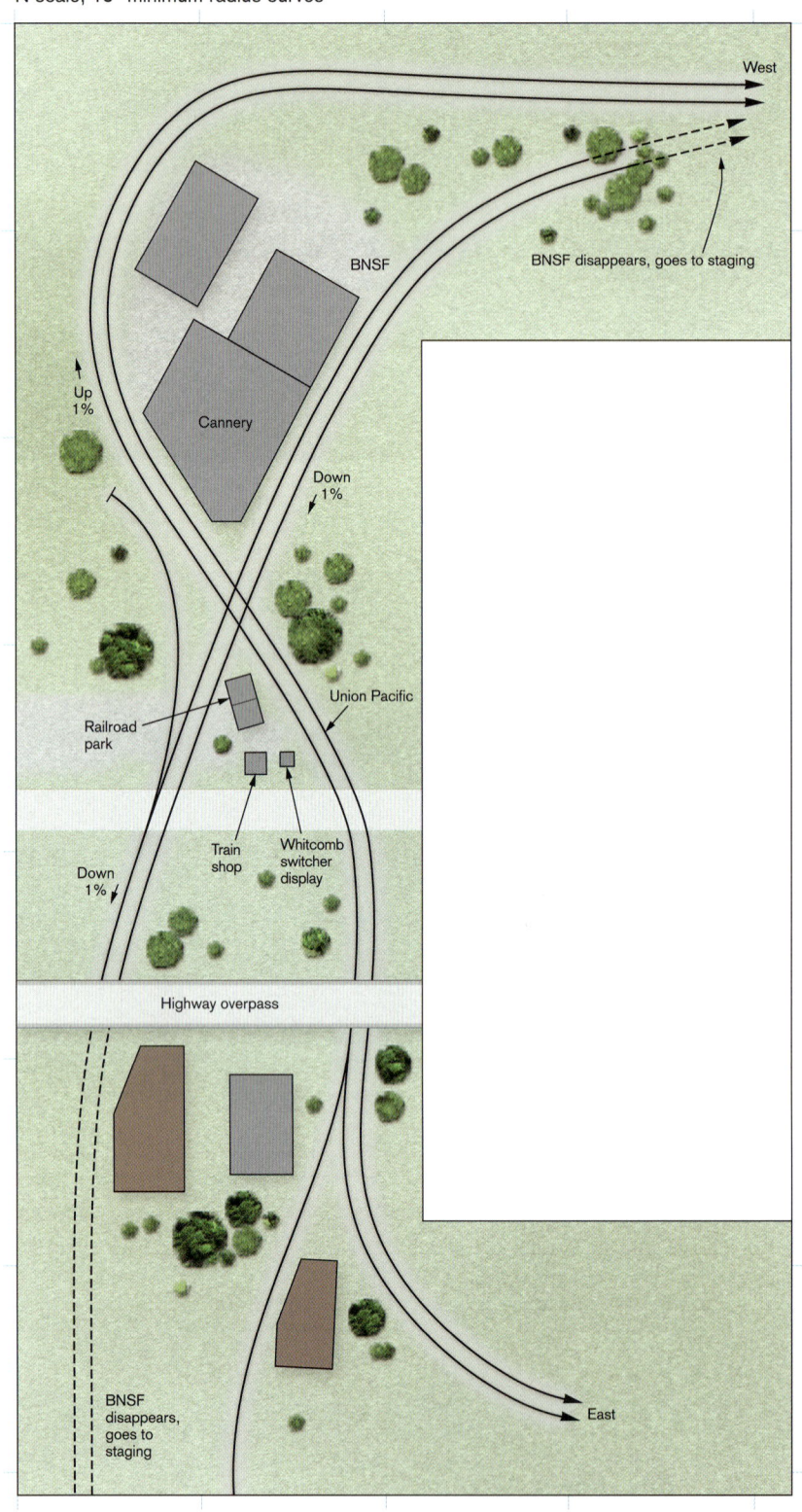

ROCHELLE, ILLINOIS
N scale, 15"-minimum-radius curves

Track plan labels:
- West
- BNSF
- BNSF disappears, goes to staging
- Up 1%
- Cannery
- Down 1%
- Railroad park
- Union Pacific
- Train shop
- Whitcomb switcher display
- Down 1%
- Highway overpass
- BNSF disappears, goes to staging
- East

A track planning concept

For the modeler who would like to sit back, relax, and watch multiple lashups of big SD90s and Dash 9s pulling quick intermodal trains interspersed with unit grain and coal trains, an N scale layout based on the Rochelle Railroad Park could offer a lot.

For me the ultimate would be hidden double-ended staging yards where I could park about ten trains for each line. Both railroads would be loops for continuous running. (Let's see ... that would require some 60 locomotives. Might have to scale that back a little.)

Again, what you did with the rest of the railroad would depend on the space you had available, how much switching you wanted, how well you like cornfields, and other personal preferences.

Just west of Rochelle, the UP has a large intermodal yard. That would certainly make a nice addition.

ALONG THE LINE

Linn H. Westcott

On the edge

Station at Bridgeport, Wis.

What do you do if your railroad runs on a riverbank with a bluff close by one side, the river itself on the other, and you need a place to put a station? The Milwaukee Road's solution at Bridgeport, Wis., was to support the station above the river bank on stilts.

Bridgeport is on the former Milwaukee Road line from Madison, Wis., to Prairie du Chien in southwestern Wisconsin. The line is now run by the Wisconsin Southern. Bridgeport is within a few miles of the Wisconsin River's confluence with the Mississippi. Unfortunately, the "bridge" in Bridgeport is only a highway bridge across the Wisconsin River.

The little station perched precariously along the main line would be an easy scratchbuilding project. Note the two sizes of horizontal siding, the lower boards appearing to be about 9" wide and the higher about 4". The six boards on the ends (and I presume the back) extend down to cover the sills on which the walls are erected. Grandt Line provides suitable doors and windows.

The clipped gables on the ends of the roof give the station a bit of a sophisticated air, and this is an easy modification you can make on just about any station kit to give your model a little different look.

If you'd rather not scratchbuild, the Depots by John no. 110 HO Country Depot has the small town look seen here. This kit is available in N as no. 6004. You could also use

The small station at Bridgeport, Wis., on the Wisconsin River is loaded with character and would be an easy scratchbuilding project.

Walthers' HO Golden Valley Depot, which comes already built in your choice of three color schemes.

Obviously, the railroad built the platform to support this station on a slope that already existed, but that's very hard to do on a model railroad if you want the result to come out neat, and above all, square. It would be much easier to build the platform on a base at your workbench and then install it and build up the scenery around it.

I'd fill in under the platform with Styrofoam packing "peanuts," then cover this base with plaster gauze

KEY MATERIALS

Station/house
Grandt Line doors and windows
Depots by John no. 110 HO country depot kit; no. 6004 in N
Walthers HO Golden Valley Depot (preassembled in choice of three color schemes)
Model Power no. 484 moving-in house

Bedsheet
Crinkled and white-painted aluminum foil

Seedy trailer
NuComp trailers, nos. 871008 or 871009 in HO; nos. 608 and 609 in N

Scenery materials/tools
Plaster gauze Woodland Scenics or Activa plaster gauze
Sculptamold
Pallette knife

Lumberyard
Atlas no. 750 HO lumberyard
Walthers no. 3057 Walton & Sons Lumber Co.; no. 3235 in N

(available from Woodland Scenics or Activa). Then I'd use a pallette knife to carefully work Sculptamold up and around the posts. Unlike plaster, Sculptamold applies very neatly, and you won't smear it on the model.

You have to like the way the house next door is built on a lower level with its entrance on the second floor, sort of a split-level home built long before they became fashionable.

Three-story house kits are hard to find. I'd buy two inexpensive plastic house kits (Model Power's no. 484 Moving-in House would work well), then kitbash. The leftovers could be used to build the garage/outbuilding.

The homeowner must have a great view of the river, and I'll bet he had a dock and a boat. The humble structure next door must serve as a garage for his car. And you wouldn't want to forget that bedsheet hanging out on the line. I'd use the old Earl Smallshaw trick. Cut the sheet from aluminum foil, crinkle it a bit, and paint it white. (If you need a prototype, pull a sheet off your bed and measure it.)

Your imagination could have a field day if you turned this scene around and built it with the river in the foreground. I don't think I could resist the temptation to add a seedy "trailer down by the river" for Matt Foley (Chris Farley's *Saturday Night Live* motivational speaker). Either of NuComp's 1950s HO trailers, nos. 871008 or 871009, would be perfect for this. You'd want to rust and dirty them up.

NuComp has similar trailers in N scale, nos. 608 and 609. Matt could park his car (a large, rusty, beat-up

Linn H. Westcott

There are plenty of kits on the market to suggest a credible representation of the real thing.

sedan) up by the lumberyard and walk down to his home.

Note the small lumberyard on up the line. The classic Atlas no. 750 HO lumberyard would be great for this. You could also use a Walthers no. 3057 Walton & Sons Lumber Co., although you'd need only one side of it and could use the rest elsewhere on the layout. Walton & Sons is also available in N scale as kit no. 3235.

Three guiding principles

Form, color, and texture

This is the kind of book that really has no end; it just runs out of pages. We have to stop somewhere, though, so for me a fine place to disembark is at Bealeville siding in Tehachapi Pass. There's no structure or bridge here to focus on as a modeling project, just a scene that promises to go on forever and instills the urge to see what lies beyond the bend.

This book has been about developing our powers of observation, looking at scenes that were preserved on film, and distilling out those elements that make them timeless so that we can re-create them in miniature. The better we can do that, the better we can re-create the experience of having been there for ourselves and for our friends. We can step into those scenes.

My old friend Bob Hayden has long been fond of saying that to build successful models, you need

Bealeville siding in Tehachapi Pass, one of the author's favorite prototype sites.

to get three things right: form, color, and texture. If those are right, then everything is right, or as artists like to say, it "works." Of course, getting those three things right can be quite a challenge.

And on that rather philosophical note, it's time to say goodbye.

Suppliers

The following is a list of many of the suppliers and manufacturers referred to throughout this book. Though we provide addresses and other information here, many of these companies do not sell direct to consumers, so we recommend that the first place you go for help in locating materials and kits is your local hobby shop. Another excellent source for model railroad equipment and materials is the annual catalog produced by the Wm. K. Walthers Co.

Details/parts/modeling materials

Activa Products PO Box 1296, 512 S. Garrett, Marshall, TX 75670, (800) 255-1910, www.activaproducts.com

Alpine Division Scale Models PO Box 6, Artesia, CA 90702-0006, (562) 860-6060, www.mria.org/companies/AlpineDivision.html

American Art Clay Co. Inc. 4717 W. 16th St., Indianapolis, IN 46222, (317) 244-6871/ (800) 374-1600, www.amaco.com

Campbell Scale Models Box 5307, Durango, CO 81303, (970) 385-7729

Cibolo Crossing PO Box 2640, Universal City, TX 78148-1640, (210) 658-4548

Environmental Technology Inc. (ETI) South Bay Depot Road, Fields Landing, CA 95537, (707) 443-9323, www.eti-usa.com

Evergreen Scale Models 18620-F 141st Ave. NE, Woodinville, WA 98072, (425) 402-4918/(877) 376-9099

Grandt Line Products 1040B Shary Ct., Concord, CA 94518, (925) 671-0806

JAKS Industries PO Box 654, Broomfield, CO 80038-0654, (303) 279-2253/(800) 352-1554, www.jaksind.com

Kappler Mill & Lumer Co. 8908 108th St. NE, Arlington, WA 98223, (888) 811-1011, www.kapplerusa.com

Kibri GMBH Postfach 1540, D-71005, Boblingen, Germany www.kibri.com

K&S Engineering 6917 W. 59th St., Chicago, IL 60638, (773) 586-8503 www.ksmetals.com

Micro Engineering Inc. 1120 Eagle Road, Fenton, MO 63026, (636) 349-1112/(800) 462-6975

Micro-Mark Precision Tools 340 Snyder Ave., Berkeley Heights, NJ 07922, (908) 464-2984/(800) 225-1066, www.micromark.com

Period Miniatures (see **JAKS Industries**)

Plastruct Inc. 1020 S. Wallace Place, City of Industry, CA 91748, (626) 912-7016/(800) 666-7015, www.plastruct.com

Scale Link Farrington, Dorset, DT11 8RA, UK, www.scalelink.co.uk

Slater Plastikard Ltd. Temple Road, Matlock Bath, Matlock, Derbyshire DE43PG, www.scalemodelindex.com/supplies-s.htm

Special Shapes 1160 Naperville Dr., Box 7487, Romeoville, IL 60446, (630) 759-1970/(800) 517-4273, www.specialshapes.com

Scale Structures Ltd. (See **JAKS Industries**)

Stewart Products LLC S-2083 Herwig Road, Reedsburg, WI 53959, (608) 254-4382

Tichy Train Group PO Box 39, Plainview, NY 11803-0039, (516) 932-3921

U.S. Gypsum Company www.gypsumsolutions.com

Williams Bros. Inc. 1119 Los Olivos Ave. #3, Los Osos, CA 93402, (805) 534-1307, www.williamsbrosinc.com

Wm. K. Walthers Inc. 5601 W. Florist Ave., Box 3039, Milwaukee, WI 53201-3039, (414) 527-0770/ (800) 877-7171, www.walthers.com

Woodland Scenics PO Box 98, Linn Creek, MO 65052, (573) 346-5555, www.woodlandscenics.com

Structures

Alpine Division Scale Models (See listing under Details/parts/modeling materials)

American Limited Models Box 7803, Fremont, CA 94537-7803, (510) 796-5593, http://americanlimitedmodels.com

American Model Builders 1420 Hanley Industrial Ct., St. Louis, MO 63144, (314) 968-3076, www.laserkit.com

American Models 10087 Colonial Industrial Dr., South Lyon, MI 48178, (248) 437-6800, www.americanmodels.com

Atlas Model Railroad Co. 378 Florence Ave., Hillside, NJ 07205, (908) 687-0880/(800) TRACK-A-1, www.atlasrr.com

Bachmann Trains 1400 E. Erie Ave., Philadelphia, PA 19124, (215) 533-1600, www.bachmanntrains.com

Craftsman Specialty Supply 6567 40-Mile Point, Rogers City, MI 49779

Depots by John PO Box 210674, Milwaukee, WI 53221-0674

Dimi Trains PO Box 1290, Verdi, NV 89439, (775) 345-6500/(800) 448-8793, www.dimitrains.com

Dyna Models 420 Flanders Road, Sangerville, ME 04479, (207) 564-7954

Funaro & Camerlengo/ Funaro Scale Models RR #5 Box 5290, Honesdale, PA 18431, (570) 224-4989

Gebr. Faller GMBH Kreuzstrasse 9, D78148, Gutenbach/Schwarzwald, Germany, 011-49-7723-651-0, www.Faller.de

IHC (International Hobby Corp.) 413 E. Allegheny Ave., Philadelphia, PA 19134-2322, (215) 426-2873/ (800) 875-1600, www.IHC-hobby.com

Model Power 180 Smith St., Farmingdale, NY 11735, (631) 694-7133/(800) 628-2803, www.modelpower.com

Northeastern Scale Models Inc. 3030 Thorntree Dr. #5, Chico, CA 95973, (530) 896-0801/(800) 840-0028, www.nesm.com

Pikestuff (See **Rix Products**)

Pola GMBH (See **Gebr. Faller GMBH**)

Rix Products 3747 Hogue Road, Evansville, IN 47712, (812) 426-1749, www.rixproducts.com

Sheepscot Scale Products 2 Country Charm Road, Cumberland, ME 04021, (207) 829-5134, http://www.sheepscotscale.com

Showcase Miniatures PO Box 753, Cherry Valley, CA 92223, (909) 845-9914

Stewart Products LLC (See listing under Details/parts/ modeling materials)

Wm. K. Walthers (See listing under Details/parts/ modeling materials)

Trestles/bridges

Atlas Model Railroad Co. (See listing under Structures)

Central Valley Model Works 1203 Pike Lane, Box 979, Oceano, CA 93445, (805) 489-8586

Gebr. Faller GMBH (See listing under Structures)

Micro Engineering (See listing under Details/parts/ modeling materials)

Model Railroad Stoneworks PMB 13235 Summit Square Center, Rt. 413 & Doublewoods Road, Langhorne, PA 19047, (215) 321-1331, www.modelrailroadstoneworks.com

Rix Products (See listing under Structures)

Tunnels

Woodland Scenics (See listing under Details/parts/ modeling materials)

Vehicles/equipment

GHQ 28100 Woodside Road, Shorewood, MN 55331, (612) 374-2693, www.ghqmodels.com

NuComp Miniatures PO Box 539, Bluffton, IN 46714, (260) 824-4820, www.nucompinc.com

Wm. K. Walthers (See listing under Details/parts/ modeling materials)

Walls

Chooch Enterprises Box 217, Redmond, WA 98052, (425) 788-8680, www.choochenterprises.com

Gebr. Faller GMBH (See listing under Structures)

Kibri GMBH (See listing under Details/parts/ modeling materials)

Noch GMBH & Co. Lindauer Str. 49, PO Box 1454, 88239 Wangen im Allgäu, Germany, 011-0049-75-2297-800, www.noch.de

Rix Products (See listing under Structures)

Woodland Scenics (See listing under Details/parts/ modeling materials)

Suggested Reading

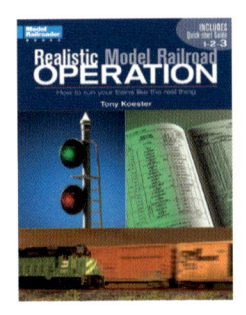

Realistic Model Railroad Operation, no. 12231. Perhaps one of the hobby's best-known authors, *MR* columnist Tony Koester, has written this comprehensive guide to operating a model railroad as though it were the real thing. Much of the information Tony include relates to yard design and arrangement so you can operate your trains in a logical, realistic manner.

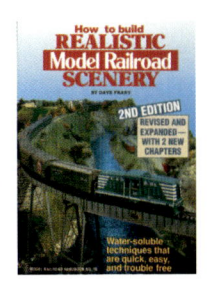

The Model Railroader's Guide to Intermodal Equipment & Operations, no. 12190. If you're modeling the more-recent railroad scene, you'll want to have an intermodal yard on your layout. This book will give you all the background behind operations and make suggestions on how to model these modern facilities.

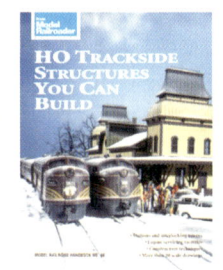

How to Build Realistic Model Railroad Scenery, no. 12100. While not directly related to the content of this book, it would be almost impossible to build a credible layout without using the techniques described in this book. You'll learn how to model the water that flows beneath your bridges, the trees that grow between industrial sites, and the rock outcroppings that overhang the right-of-way. This is the classic book on the subject of scenery for your model railroad.

HO Trackside Structures You Can Build, no. 12143. Similar to no. 12168, *Trackside Structures* focuses on railroad stations, yard structures, and engine-servicing facilities—those buildings necessary to keep a railroad running. The 18 projects include photos, plans, and instructions to guide you through the process of adding railroad structures to your layout.

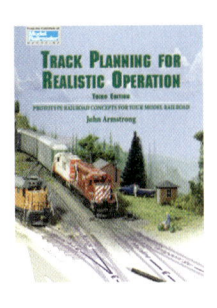

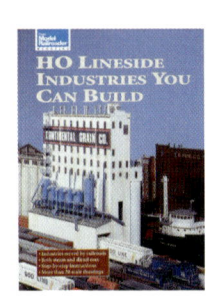

Track Planning for Realistic Operation, no. 12148. John Armstrong's book is a classic in the hobby. Like Tony Koester's book, *Realistic Model Railroad Operation*, Armstrong sets out to teach his readers everything they need to know about how real railroads operate so they can build a realistic model railroad. Where you place switches, for instance, makes a big difference! The book includes lots of track diagrams of railroad yards with explanations of why they're arranged the way they are.

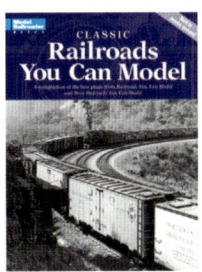

HO Lineside Industries You Can Build, no. 12168. Featuring classic articles from *Model Railroader* Magazine, this book shows how to build and detail the industries served by both steam- and diesel-era railroads, including factories, warehouses, scrapyards, oil depots, lumberyards, and other industrial facilities. Most articles include photos of the real structure, provide drawings to help you with your models, and include step-by-step instructions and photos illustrating how to build the structure for your layout.

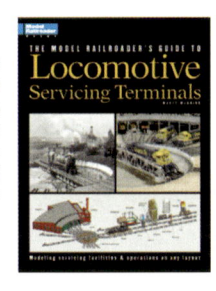

Classic Railroads You Can Model, no. 12238. It all starts with the track plan. If you want your model railroad to give the illusion of reality, why not start out with reality. This book of classic track plans from *Model Railroader* Magazine is based on the premise of starting with a real location or stretch of railroad and building a model railroad that captures the key features of that area.

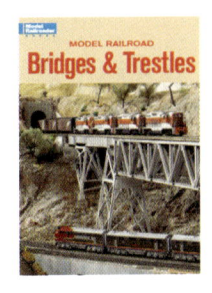

The Model Railroader's Guide to Locomotive Servicing Terminals, no. 12228. This terrific guide has information applicable to almost anyone who builds a model railroad. Written by former *MR* associate editor Marty McGuirk, the book covers both steam- and diesel-era servicing facilities, including drawings and photos of real railroad structures as well as modeling tips for many of the facilities.

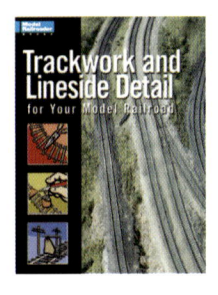

Model Railroad Bridges & Trestles, no. 12101. Another standard book in the hobby, *Bridges & Trestles* provides more than 20 sets of drawings that show you how to build credible plate girder bridges, through-truss bridges, viaducts, timber trestles, and many more structures designed to convey railroads over dips in the terrain or water.

Trackwork and Lineside Detail for your Model Railroad, no. 12235. The first half of this book includes detailed instruction on how to lay track, useful information for anyone building a layout. The second half is more in keeping with the subject of this book. Articles, many of them written by *MR*'s associate editor Gordon Odegard, include information on such railroad details as bumping posts, bridge guard rails, switch stands, line poles, whistle posts, and a dozen more. Included with each item are drawings and photos to help you with your modeling.

Tourist Trains
This annual directory of tourist railroads and model railroads open to the public gives you all the information you'll need to find the location, costs, hours, etc., of nearly 400 operations in the U.S. and Canada. By visiting these railroads, riding the trains, and keeping your eyes open, you'll find yourself better equipped to build a model railroad that looks and operates like the real thing!

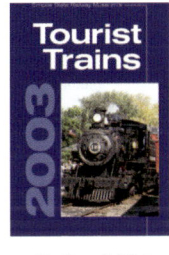

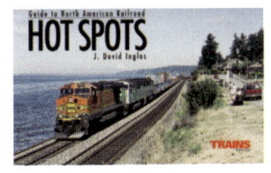

Building City Scenery for Your Model Railroad, no. 12204. Railroads generally run from one city to the next and beyond, so most model railroads will need to represent an urban scene in some way. This book offers many tips on how to assemble and place buildings to suggest a big city without actually having to build a big city.

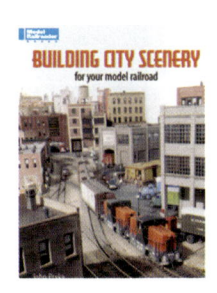

Guide to North American Railroad Hot Spots, no. 01097. Nothing increases your chances of building a realistic model railroad than observing real railroads. This guide provides color photos of the 100 best trainwatching sites, along with directions how to get there, and information about the railroad activity you're likely to see.

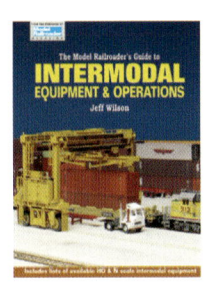

Index

Access roads, ... 59
Backdrops, ... 60-61, 63
BNSF, ... 71-74
Bridges,
    deck girder, . . . 33-34, 38-39, 42-44, 63, 64, 65
    deck truss, ... 38-39, 63
    foot, ... 13
    lift, ... 55
    steel through-truss, ... 45-46
    steel trestle, ... 38-41, 60-61
    stone, ... 30-35, 63
    swing, ... 45, 52-54
Buffalo & Pittsburgh, ... 21, 38-39
Burlington Northern, ... 14, 41, 60-61, 62
Chicago & Illinois Midland, ... 26-27
Chicago & North Western, ... 10-12, 16-17, 43
Clinchfield Railroad, ... 15
Coal operations, ... 12-13
Conrail, ... 32, 63, 64
CSX, ... 63
Cuts, ... 34, 62, 66-68
Detroit, Toledo & Ironton, ... 18-19
Diamonds, track, ... 71-72
Enginehouses, ... 22-29
Fuel facilities, ... 19-20, 21, 22, 23, 26
Illinois Central, ... 45-51
Intermodal operations, ... 14

Lincoln, Abraham, ... 51
Louisville & Nashville, ... 12
Milwaukee, Racine & Troy, ... 40-41
Milwaukee Road, ... 24, 75-76
Mississippi River crossings, ... 45-55
Norfolk Southern, ... 22, 52-55
Overpasses, highway, ... 8, 10-11
Pennsylvania Railroad, ... 30-37
Rail bumpers, ... 19, 27, 69
Rio Grande, ... 65
Sand towers, ... 18-19,22
Santa Fe, ... 6-7, 42,43, 56-59, 66-70, 77
Shed, warm-up, ... 9
Signals, ... 72
Southern Pacific, ... 43, 56-59, 66-70, 77
Stations, ... 75-76
Tehachapi Pass, ... 43, 56-59, 66-70, 77
Towers, railroad, ... 9
Track planning concepts, ... 50, 70, 74
Tunnels, ... 13, 47-50, 54, 57-59, 66-68
Turntables, ... 25, 29
Union Pacific, ... 71-74
Wabash Railroad, ... 52-54
Water, ... 36-37, 38-39, 43, 64, 75
Weathering, ... 8-17
Winifrede Railroad, ... 23
Yards, ... 6-17